Anxiety

Reaching A State Of Mental Serenity May Help Relieve
Stress And Anxiety And Enjoy Your Life With A Fresh
Dose Of Happiness And Self Assurance

(By Focusing On The Here And Now, You May Free
Yourself From The Burden Of Unnecessary Reflection)

MelquiadesOropeza

TABLE OF CONTENT

Introduction 1

Adopting Thought Patterns And Beliefs That Are Harmful To Oneself And Others 5

The Terror That Comes From Unknowing 10

The Connection Between An Individual's Physical Health And Mental State Of Mind 14

Keeping Your Strength Up While You Are Going Through The Recovery Process To You From Falling Back Into Old Habits. 21

Why Is It Essential To Have A High Level Of Emotional Intelligence In Order To Experience Positive Feelings About Oneself? 27

The Ability To Exert Control Over One's Breathing Is Essential To Reaching A State Of Calm 30

Confronting The Facts And Occurrences Of The World 41

Taking Responsibility For Your Path To Achieving Inner Calm 54

True Stories Of The Struggles And Triumphs Against Anxiety Experienced By Regular People In Everyday Life. 58

What Precisely Is Meant By The Term "Sleep Anxiety"? 66

Help Your Child Overcome Their Social Anxiety By Giving Them Your Support. 69

Attempt To Retain Mastery Over Your Powerful Emotionssomeone 78

How To Preserve Your Own Internal Calm 84

Improving Both Physical And Emotional Intimacy With The Help Of Direction 100

The Struggle With Anxiety And How Mindfulness Can Help 107

Building Mental Fortitude And Focus Will Help You Focus And Be More Resilient. 111

The Role That Each Gene Plays In The Development Of The Anxiety Condition 123

In The Event That You Have Social Anxiety Disorder, There Are Specific Actions That You Ought To Steer Clear Of. 132

Put An End To The Delusion That You Are The Only One Who Is Going Through This. 142

Introduction

Because Our Bodies Have Evolved To Respond In This Way To A Variety Of Stimuli, Including Possible Triggers For Anxiety, We All Experience Episodes Of Worry And Anxiety From Time To Time. This Is Because Our Bodies Have Evolved To Respond In This Way To A Variety Of Stimuli. However, The Vast Majority Of Us Are Able To Regain Our Typical Level Of Composure Once A Certain Amount Of Time Has Passed Since The Traumatic Experience That Triggered Our Response. On The Other Hand, There Are Several Circumstances In Which This So-Called "Return To Normalcy" Does Not Occur As Expected. When You Have An Anxiety Disorder, All You Can Do Is Worry And Feel Terrified Of Everything. There Is Nothing Else You Can Do. Because You Are Constantly Anxious, It Looks As Though You Are Unable To Get Things Done, And Even When You Do Get Things Done, You Are Always Apprehensive About The Results Of The Things You Have Done. This

Gives The Impression That You Are Unable To Get Things Done. As A Direct Consequence Of This, You Might Even Find That You Steer Clear Of Particular Situations, Individuals, And Even Locations. This May Then Lead To Feelings Of Isolation, Which, In The Long Run, Will Only Serve To Make Your Anxiety Worse. Are You Sick And Tired Of Living This Kind Of Life, One That Is Filled With Constant Tension And Concern? Are You Sick And Tired Of Living This Kind Of Life? Do You Want To Be Free To Pursue Your Objectives And Ambitions Without Being Hampered By Anxiety And Fear About What Other People May Think Of You? If So, This Article Is For You. Do You Want To Understand How To Reduce The Symptoms Of Your Anxiety And Put An End To Having Panic Attacks?

In The Event That This Were Not The Case, I Would Not Have Anticipated Seeing You Here Today. This Book Will Provide Additional Information On Anxiety, The Various Categories Of Anxiety, And The Ways In Which You Can Evaluate Yourself To Decide Whether Or Not You Have A Problem With Anxiety. You Will Also Learn How To Identify The Triggers That Cause Your Anxiety, As Well As How To Respond

To Them And Build Skills For Managing With The Worry That They Cause. You Will Also Acquire An Understanding Of How The Way You Live Your Life May Be Contributing To The Severity Of Your Anxiety, As Well As What Changes You May Make In Order To Better Manage Your Anxiety. This Knowledge Is In Addition To The Fact That You Will Learn What Changes You May Do In Order To Better Manage Your Anxiety.

This Book Will Not Try To Steer You In Any One Direction Regarding The Three Different Avenues That Are Open To You. Give Yourself Permission To Choose Your Own Action. Think About Both Your Advantages And The Resources You Have Available, And Then Base Your Decision On The Analysis You Just Did.

Also, Keep In Mind That You Always Have The Opportunity To Change Your Mind, Even If You Have Every Intention Of Going Along A Particular Course Of Action. This Is An Important Thing To Keep In Mind Because It Is Easy To Forget That You Always Have This Option. If You Are Working With A Professional And You Do Not Get The Outcomes You Want, You May Be Open And Honest About The Fact That You Want To Try Helping Yourself By Utilizing Self-Help

Approaches. This Is Something You Can Do Even If You Are Not Getting The Results You Want From Working With The Expert. Or, If You Opted To Pursue The Option Of Self-Help But, At Some Point, You Realized That You Had Reached A Dead End And Were Unable To Handle Things On Your Own, You Should Not Be Afraid To Schedule An Appointment With A Qualified Medical Professional. Maintain An Open Line Of Communication With The Expert Regarding How You Managed The Predicament, The Techniques You Utilized, And The Results You Obtained. It Has Commonly Been Discovered That The Most Effective Method For Resolving Challenges Is To Use A Combination Of Strategies That Are Targeted Toward Self-Help, In Addition To The Occasional (And Only If Absolutely Necessary) Aid Of A Trained Specialist. This Has Been Found To Be The Most Effective Method.

Adopting Thought Patterns And Beliefs That Are Harmful To Oneself And Others

Many of us, in the same way that some of us participate in avoidance behaviors as a means of coping with social anxiety, also resort to negative ideas as a method of helping us to cope with our anxiety. This is because we believe that negative views are more helpful than positive beliefs. In certain ways, we have a tendency to make the mistaken assumption that if we are critical of ourselves, it will help ease some of the pain that is created by the behavior of others toward us that is (supposed to be) expected. These views are generally the result of having a low sense of self-esteem, certain experiences from the individual's history, avoidance, and impostor syndrome.

Take into account the points that are listed below. You probably already have some notion of how excruciatingly dreadful it can be to go through a humiliating incident, especially if you have gone through it in the past or if you grew up being ridiculed for something. If either of these situations applies to you, then you probably already have some understanding of how excruciatingly awful it can be. In order to protect yourself, you will most likely devise reasons for that kind of behavior. These explanations will most likely involve blaming yourself for the behavior in question. Alternately, you may play out detailed scenarios in your imagination concerning what might go on when you put yourself out there in order to get yourself ready for the various results that are possible. The following is an example of some of the negative thoughts that we could employ as a means of coping with our social anxiety: There is something fundamentally flawed about me; I'm a broken person; people don't find me likeable. My nervousness, anxiety, and/or awkwardness are readily apparent to those around me. I don't have anything to contribute to the conversation, and I don't think anything I say will add anything of value to it either. I am unable to add anything to the discussion, nor do I anticipate being in a position to offer anything of value to the discussion. It is just a matter of time before I completely disgrace myself in front of other people or make a fool of myself in front of other people.

The problem is that when you beat yourself up in this fashion, you could get a short feeling of relief since it implies that you don't have to put your social abilities to the test or even be a part of social situations. This, however, is not a healthy way to think about the situation because it really makes the problem worse. These beliefs, however, can make it more difficult for you to overcome your social anxiety because they are similar to the avoidance and safety behaviors that you participate in. This is because these beliefs are rooted in the idea that you are a bad person. What's more, some of these ideas can even serve as self-fulfilling prophecies, which means that you can end up behaving in a way that makes you feel as if your worst thoughts about yourself are true. This is because self-fulfilling prophecies cause you to act in a way that makes your beliefs about yourself come true. This is something that might occur if a person has negative thoughts about themselves and then goes on to behave in a way that reinforces those thoughts.

A Lack of Confidence in Oneself Along with Negative Thoughts About Oneself

I would like to approach this topic in an autonomous manner despite the fact that it is tied to detrimental notions and ways of thinking. One of the key factors that plays a role in women having a harder time dealing with issues related to low self-esteem is the fact that they are expected to perform better in some facets of their lives. For instance, it is expected of women that they will always come across as affable and pleasant, and that they would never publicly reveal indications of distress. Another expectation is that men will always appear to be affable and nice. In addition to this, there is the expectation that women should be "perfect" in some positions, such as that of a mother. The assumption that women should constantly appear "put-together" might lead to them experiencing an increasing sense of being treated as "social objects" when their number of social contacts increases. This is because the expectation that women should always seem "put-together" As a consequence of this, people might give more consideration to the impression that they provide to other folks.

Girls are generally subjected to a range of expectations regarding their behavior and looks, and these expectations can come from their mothers, aunts, and other female family elders. This can be a burdensome experience for girls. What's even worse is that the person who is the focus of these rebukes or reprimands may, over time, wind up internalizing them as part of their own identity. It's likely that we won't be able to differentiate between the sound of our own voices and the voices of other people. When we begin to accept the fact that there is a voice within our heads that tells us, "You're never going to be good enough," we may begin to avoid situations in which we might be able to demonstrate that the voice is right. This may occur when we begin to accept the idea that there is a voice within our heads that tells us, "You're never going to be good enough." Also, perfection cannot be achieved because it is impossible; therefore, we are fighting a battle against ourselves that we cannot win, which only helps to make our worry worse over time. Also, perfection cannot be achieved because it is impossible.

Low self-esteem can have a lot of unfavorable impacts on women, one of which is sending the message that we do not deserve to get well or accept aid. This is only one of the many harmful repercussions that can occur. It sends the message that we are liable for everything that is happening to us and that we are deserving of everything that is happening to us because we are responsible for it in some manner. This not only delays therapy (if it is required), but it also helps us feel more at ease despite the stressful situation we are in.

The Terror That Comes From Unknowing

The Six Fundamental Needs of Human Beings serve as the overarching foundation for all of our ideas, deeds, and patterns of behavior. These needs can be broken down into three categories: physiological, psychological, and social. Many of us yearn for certainty above all else; we want to be informed of everything that is going to take place in the future.

Even if there must be some degree of predictability in our lives, there must also be some degree of unpredictability and variation.

It is much less probable that we will venture outside of our safety zones when we are plagued with anxiety about the unknown.

The message that has been conveyed to us is, "You might as well stay here, where it's safe." It is the primary reason why so many people have the perception that they are unable to achieve their objectives and objectives in life.

THE TERROR THAT COMES WITH SUCCESS

The human need for certainty as well as the need to be important are both contributors to the universal fear that people experience, which is the fear that they will be unsuccessful in what it is that they are attempting to do.

We are hardwired to seek pleasure and avoid pain, and avoiding failure is without a doubt one of the most straightforward ways to steer clear of being miserable. In spite of the fact that we want to make a positive difference in the world, failure has a way of making us feel insignificant and trivial.

On the other hand, we are also hardwired for growth, and as any person who has achieved success in their life is aware, the path to advancement is paved with a series of setbacks along the way. You have to reframe how you think about failure so that you see it as something great rather than something dreadful. If you do this, you will be able to overcome your fear of failure.

HOW TO BECOME VICTORIOUS IN YOUR BATTLE AGAINST FEAR

Conquering fear needs you to take control of the fear reaction and figure out how to use it to your advantage. If you want to conquer fear, you need to do both of these things. The first thing you need to do in order to acquire the art of conquering fear is to find your center.

The next piece will present you with tried-and-true strategies for overcoming fear and anxiety so that you can take pleasure in every moment of your life.

BE AWARE OF YOUR OWN ANXIETIES AND FEARS

Learning how to conquer one's fears is like to learning how to solve any other kind of difficulty in the sense that one must first identify the obstacle before attempting to overcome it. This is true whether one is learning how to tackle a fear of spiders or a fear of heights.

What exactly are you so terrified of that causes you to feel this way? Spend some time meditating on the thoughts, emotions, and physical sensations that are currently running through your head and body. Take a few minutes to sit quietly. Take notes on everything you find, and strive to be as descriptive as you can in your writing.

Establishing and maintaining a consistent mindfulness meditation practice can be beneficial in a number of ways, one of which is the attainment of a more thorough insight into the factors that drive one. You will gain a sense of agency as you move closer to finding who you truly are, which will empower you to address your concerns as you progress along this path.

The Connection Between An Individual's Physical Health And Mental State Of Mind

When examining the phenomenon of concern, the significance of the connection between the mind and the body cannot be exaggerated because of the strong connection that exists between the two.

The following is a list of the physical impacts that anxiety has on a person: Anxiety is known to be the root cause of a wide range of physical symptoms, some of which include a racing heartbeat, shallow breathing, tense muscles, and digestive issues. Teenagers who are aware that the above-mentioned physical manifestations are indicators of anxiousness and are able to better manage their condition as a result may reap the benefits of this treatment.

Why Engaging in Physical Activity Is So Important: Endorphins are natural mood boosters produced by the body, and research has shown that engaging in regular physical activity can help ease anxiety by releasing endorphins. One strategy that can be helpful in the management of anxiety in teenagers is to encourage them to participate in physical activity. This can be done in a number of different ways.

Food and drink consumed, as well as nutrition: The foods that a person consumes can have an influence, not only on their mood, but also on the amount of anxiety that they feel. Eating a diet that is rich in fruits, vegetables, whole grains, and lean meats can significantly improve both an individual's mental and physical health.

Anxiety with a Disrupted Sleep Pattern: There is some evidence that suggests that poor sleep quality or not getting enough sleep can make anxiety symptoms worse. The development of healthy sleeping habits that allow for sufficient amounts of restful sleep is a crucial component of anxiety management for teenagers.

The Relationship That Exists Between the Mind and the Body Techniques such as mindfulness, yoga, and deep breathing exercises can help adolescents feel more connected to their bodies and have less anxious thoughts by reducing the effects of stress on the mind and body. These techniques are useful for relaxing and gaining emotional mastery since they help one put their feelings under control.

A holistic approach, which can be offered by an awareness of the relationship between a person's physical and mental health, may prove to be beneficial in the treatment of teen anxiety. Teenagers can get started on the path toward greater stability and resiliency if they pay attention to the signals that their bodies are providing them and simultaneously take care of their physical and mental well-being.

How can you prevent yourself from dwelling on irrelevant details?

It's conceivable that you're giving too much thought to the current predicament. On the other hand, there is absolutely no cause for anxiety regarding this matter. It is natural to sometimes give something more attention than it warrants, but this does not mean that it is abnormal to do so. It's not unusual to give too much thought to things. Because it is present, both the processing of information and the solution of issues are facilitated, with the former facilitating the latter. On the other side, when we dwell on a subject for an excessive amount of time, we frequently discover that we are unable to escape feelings of uneasiness, concern, or tension.

Try some of these strategies to put an end to your habit of overthinking if you feel as though you are thinking more than is customary for you.

1. Allocate some time specifically for your own relaxation. Get some exercise, breathe in some clean air, and spend some time doing something fun outside, like going for a walk.

2. Pay close attention to the activity in which you are presently participating.

3. While you are working on whatever it is that you are currently working on, think about how you will respond once you have completed it, as well as how it will make you feel. You can boost your ability to think by engaging in excessive mental activity. It is natural to go through phases in which you overthink things to an

unhealthy degree. Sometimes we need to take some time to think and reflect on our sentiments, and other times we need to just let go of our feelings and thoughts completely. Sometimes we need to take some time to think and reflect on our feelings.

4. The less likely it is that you will actually do something, the more time you spend thinking about it, and the more time you spend thinking about it, the less likely it is that you will actually do it. If you are thinking about doing anything, there is a good chance that you won't end up actually doing what you're thinking about doing. This is because whenever you start thinking about doing something, your brain immediately begins to prepare itself to carry out the notion that you are thinking about doing. Therefore, even if you don't end up carrying out what you were considering doing, you feel compelled to do it anyhow due to the fact that you feel obligated to do it.

5. If you let something happen when you aren't paying attention to it, it will happen nonetheless.

That's exactly as it should be! When we give a certain action our whole attention, we increase the possibility that we will actually carry it through. The instant we even think about doing anything, our brains immediately begin to prepare themselves for it. This is true regardless of what it is that we are considering doing. If you tell yourself when you wake up, "I really need to go to the gym today," then there is a good probability that you will actually end up going to the gym.

The ability to think clearly is beneficial to one's overall health.

If someone tells you that you overthink things, it's probable that you won't believe them just because they said it. This is understandable. All you are doing, in the end, is trying to find out what steps to take when this one is over. On the other hand, there is evidence to suggest that participating in a great deal of mental thinking can assist one in making better decisions.

There are many reasons for overthinking, as well as many catalysts that launch the undesirable behaviors of overthinking, which can lead to anxiety and excessive worrying if they are not stopped. If these behaviors are not stopped, overthinking can cause anxiety and excessive worrying. One of the most typical motivations for engaging in excessive mental processing is the worry that one would overlook a vital detail. These are not pleasant sensations, and something that at first appears to be prudent caution and cautious contemplation can very soon develop into something that is far more serious and can have catastrophic effects.

Keeping Your Strength Up While You Are Going Through The Recovery Process To You From Falling Back Into Old Habits.

The path to recovery is a journey that is filled with both successes and challenges at various points along the way. It is crucial to keep in mind that there is always a chance of falling back into old habits. While recognising the accomplishments accomplished in overcoming addiction can be a source of motivation and empowerment, it is also important to bear in mind that there is always a risk of relapsing. Relapse, often known as returning to substance use after a period of sobriety, is a common occurrence that can be highly unpleasant for someone who is in the process of recovering from substance abuse.

However, if one is armed with the necessary knowledge and skills, it is possible to prevent relapse and continue on the path towards a life that is fulfilling while they are in the process of recovering from their addiction.

The Method of Locating Inciting Circumstances

A relapse can occur as a result of a chain reaction of cravings, which can be referred to as a trigger. A trigger can be an event, a setting, or a mood that kicks off this chain reaction. Common triggers include things like stress, boredom, bad feelings, negative emotions, pressure from peers, and being exposed to the substance of choice. On the other hand, they can be rather different from one person to the next.

Keeping a journal or making a note of your thoughts and feelings at various points throughout the day may be helpful in discovering the elements that are the specific triggers for your own unique reactions. This can help you become more aware of patterns and situations that may lead to cravings and give you more control over them. It can also help you become more aware of patterns and situations that may contribute to cravings. In addition, seeking support from therapists, sponsors, or support groups can provide extra insight into identifying triggers and finding techniques to cope with them. This can be quite helpful in the recovery process.

Developing a Plan to Avoid Making Mistakes in the Future

After you have identified the factors that contribute to your relapses, the following stage is to devise a plan to stop such episodes from occurring in the future. This might include strategies for avoiding or coping with triggers, as well as steps to take in the event that a relapse occurs when an individual is in the process of recovering from an addiction.

Participating in self-care practices and ways for managing stress, such as going for regular workouts, practicing meditation, and maintaining a nutritious diet, are common methods for preventing relapse and should be used whenever possible. It is also vital to have a support system in place for times when you are feeling vulnerable and to avoid situations or individuals that may trigger cravings. In addition, it is crucial to have a support system in place for times when you are feeling vulnerable. It may be helpful to avoid situations or people who are likely to provoke cravings in order to be successful.

It is vitally important to have a plan in place in the event that you experience a relapse in your recovery from an addiction. This can include asking for assistance from loved ones or professionals, going to meetings or therapy sessions, and reevaluating your coping strategies moving forward in order to better handle future challenges.

Bear in mind that a relapse is not a sign of failure but rather an opportunity to learn and grow as you continue on your path to recovery from whatever it is that caused the relapse in the first place.

Keeping up an Unwavering Dedication to the Healing Process

It can be challenging to stick to a treatment plan and keep one's commitment to sobriety when one is presented with triggers and cravings. However, it is vital to keep in mind the benefits of abstinence over the course of one's lifetime, as well as the positive influence that it may have on one's overall health and fitness.

In particular, it can be helpful to remind oneself of the motivations that led to the decision to attempt recovery in the first place, especially when things are going poorly. This could entail improving personal relationships, achieving personal goals, and leading a life that is simultaneously healthier and more happy.

It is imperative that when you find yourself in a position where you require assistance, you look for it not just from the individuals who are important to you but also from educated professionals. They will be able to offer you support, direction, and accountability all the way through the process of your recovery from whatever ailment you are battling.

In addition, continuing your success can be made easier if you engage in self-care practices and look for healthy ways to deal with stress. Participating in activities that you enjoy, making goals that are within your reach, and identifying good coping techniques for dealing with stress and other feelings are all examples of things that fall under this category.

It is important to keep in mind that getting better is a process that continues continuously, and there may be ups and downs along the way. But if you continue to be committed to your sobriety and put into action a strategy to prevent relapse, you will be able to prevail over challenges and continue on your journey toward a life that is healthier and provides you more enjoyment. In light of this, it is imperative that you do not give up, that you maintain your strength, and that you recognize that you are not alone on the path to recovery. You have the power and the determination to triumph over any obstacle that may be placed in your path because you are confident in your ability to succeed.

Why Is It Essential To Have A High Level Of Emotional Intelligence In Order To Experience Positive Feelings About Oneself?

The following is a list of some of the many reasons why emotional intelligence is important to not only our mental but also our physical health. At this point, the first and most essential reason ought to be obvious and almost self-evident: emotional intelligence enables you to comprehend your feelings to the fullest extent possible, which is a benefit that cannot be overstated. Even on a strictly quantitative and "numerical" level, it has been proved that the human brain generates more emotions than rational thinking. In turn, feelings are a very big component of your whole personality and make up a very important part of you. Furthermore, your feelings and emotions frequently function as a more strong driver of your decisions and behaviors than does your thinking. This is because your feelings and emotions are more deeply rooted in your past experiences. If you want to have a more accurate grasp of who you are and the kind of person you want to evolve into in the future, having a high emotional intelligence is without a doubt vital. These elements contribute to why having a high emotional intelligence is essential.

Emotional intelligence can also help us improve our self-confidence and self-esteem, both of which are essential life abilities. Emotional intelligence can help us build these qualities. You will be able to realize the value that you genuinely possess as well as the complexities of your own personality if you are able to understand those complications. If you don't believe me that this will assist boost your confidence, then give it a shot and see for yourself!

Lastly, but certainly not least, increasing our emotional intelligence can also assist us in generating greater empathy for the experiences of others. To be able to "read" other people as if they were open books, it is extremely beneficial to have an emotional and mental grasp of what they are going through. This is because reading other people requires empathy. If you only pay attention to someone's rational viewpoints, you will never be able to see into their heart; instead, you will need to take things one step further and concentrate on how they feel about things.

If you are capable of understanding another person's feelings, you may say with absolute certainty that you are familiar with every aspect of that person's character. Even if it is merely in a roundabout way and "reflexively," this makes a big contribution to your general wellbeing.

You should now have a clear understanding of the reasoning behind why emotional intelligence is of the utmost significance. In the next paragraph, I will finish filling in the gaps in your knowledge of emotional intelligence by expanding on the reasons why it is also crucial in professional settings. I will do this by discussing some of the reasons why emotional intelligence is important in professional settings.

The Ability To Exert Control Over One's Breathing Is Essential To Reaching A State Of Calm.

The most crucial step in lessening the severity of panic attacks and overall levels of stress is learning to manage one's breathing. This can be accomplished in a number of different ways. When we are confronted with overwhelming worry, our usual breathing rhythm frequently becomes disorganized, which, unbeknownst to us, contributes to the very sensation of dread that we are striving to ease. This puts in motion a potentially deadly loop in which anxiety increases, leaving us with the sensation of being lost in a whirlwind of feelings.

The following simple observation can help shed light on your breathing patterns: if, while inhaling, only your chest and shoulders lift, then it is conceivable that your breathing pattern is unwittingly making your stress worse. It is of the utmost importance to ensure that your abdominal muscles expand with each breath that you take in. It is a known fact that while one is in the midst of conditions that are causing worry for them, this method may appear counterintuitive or even make the suffering much worse. Toughness, on the other hand, is what separates those who succeed from those who fail. Because diaphragmatic breathing allows your nervous system to transition out of a heightened state and into a more relaxed one, it only takes a few minutes to feel like yourself again when you practice diaphragmatic breathing. This is due to the fact that the practice causes your nervous system to relax.

The rhythm of your breath is another essential component that you need to keep in mind: the duration of your exhales need to be longer than the duration of your inhales. It is strongly suggested that you take a prolonged, deep breath in through your nose, followed by a gentle exhalation through your mouth. Maintaining one's determination in the face of what could feel like an insurmountable obstacle during an anxiety attack is, nonetheless, absolutely necessary. The practice of making a soft "shhh" sound while exhaling, which naturally slows the breath and assists in the promotion of relaxation, is one piece of helpful advice that is offered by a number of specialists working in the sector.

The Importance Of Having A Good Understanding Of Where Triggers Originate

It is vital, in order to get a deeper grasp of the attachment triggers that you feel, to study the sources of the attachment triggers that are causing you to experience these symptoms. Consider the following, among other things:

Which Earlier Events Were Responsible for My Triggers' Activation? Think about the memories you have from your childhood, particularly the ones that involve your primary caregivers and the first people you interacted with. Have you ever been neglected, had inconsistency in your life, or been through any traumatic experiences that could have contributed to the formation of your triggers?

In what ways have there been past opportunities for romantic involvement in this narrative? Consider some of the things you've been through in terms of love, friendship, or the dynamics of your family in the past. Do you find that particular kinds of relationships or circumstances in your life have an effect on the attachment triggers you use?

Where did my fundamental beliefs originate, and how do they impact the way I react to certain situations?

Look into the underlying presumptions or self-perceptions that serve as the foundation for your emotional reactions. Do you, for example, believe that you are unlovable or that someone will give up on you in the future?

Gaining Mastery Over the Factors That Cause Attachment

Once you have recognized and gained an understanding of these attachment triggers, you will be in a position to take steps toward a more effective control of your attachment triggers.

Find a solution. Bear the following in mind: Mindfulness is a practice that can help you become more aware of how your thoughts and emotions are influencing you in the here and now. With the help of mindfulness, you can acquire the skills to pause, ponder, and select responses that are more suited to your needs.

Confronting Beliefs That Cannot Be Supported: Reframe your negative beliefs that are contributing to your triggers by analyzing them and changing how you think about them. It's possible that using strategies from cognitive behavioral therapy, or CBT for short, will be useful in accomplishing this objective.

Discuss the Issues at Hand With Your Husband/Wife/Partner: When you are in a relationship, having a dialogue with your spouse that is honest and open about the things that irritate you can have a transformative influence on the dynamic of the partnership. By being open and honest about your limitations and needs, you can help foster more mutual comprehension and confidence.

Make an Effort to Solicit the Help of a Professional: Think about going to therapy if the triggers of your attachments have a significant negative effect not just on your overall health but also on the quality of the relationships you have. Your therapist may be able to provide you with guidance and skills that may assist you in properly addressing and managing the triggers that you experience.

It is incredibly useful for you to have an awareness of the attachment triggers you encounter, not only for the sake of your own personal growth but also for the sake of the development of your relationships. It enables you to break free from the usual emotional responses that you ordinarily have and, instead, make conscious decisions about how you will react when confronted with hard circumstances. You may be able to increase the quality of the connections you have in your life by first determining the causes of your worry and stress and then working on creating healthy coping skills to deal with those causes.

Music for the Instruments to Help Tame the Fierce Beast

Music has a remarkable potential to change both our mental state and our level of energy in an instant, and it may do both simultaneously. The ability of a simple melody and lyric to move us emotionally, inspire us to take action, or take us to a place of rest can all be attributed to the power of music. Making use of the therapeutic properties of music is a simple and readily available treatment option for anxiety.

Make sure that the songs on your playlists convey the emotions that you want to feel at a specific point in time. If you want to have a better attitude and more motivation while you're working out or doing something else that's monotonous, listening to uplifting music with good lyrics will help. It may be good to listen to slow instrumental music or the sounds of nature when you are experiencing feelings of being overwhelmed. When the music is suited to your current state of mind as well as the activity that you are participating in, the effect of the music is increased.

When you listen to music, practicing presence entails giving the music your full and undivided attention in addition to using playlists to organize the songs you want to hear. You should make sure that you give yourself time on a daily basis to really hear the music that moves you and to experience it. You will get less out of an experience if you try to juggle too many things at once, so try to avoid doing that.

Create some racket with the musical first aid gear you have. You could find it helpful to listen to some music that is intended to calm and soothe you, such as acoustic, classical, ambient, or spiritual music. It's possible that listening to songs with an upbeat pop, rock, hip-hop, or dance beat will give you a rush of energy. It is physically impossible to feel down when belting out your favorite song, so why not take advantage of the upbeat effect that music has by singing along with it?

At live performances, the impact of the music is magnified because it is blended with the energy of the crowd that has gathered to experience it. This throng has gathered because they want to experience the music. Dancing and swaying to live music can provide one with a pleasurable experience that engages all aspects of the body. Discover low-cost venues in your neighborhood so that you can fulfill your demand for live music on a more regular basis.

Music is a versatile medium that may be utilized in a number of different ways to reach the mental state that you want to have. It is not difficult to transport, it will not put a significant dent in your finances, and it is available at the touch of a button around the clock. Continue to experiment with your own individualized playlists and activities to determine which ones bring out the best in music's power to calm anxious feelings.

Now, let's have a look at some particular musical strategies that can assist in the reduction of anxiety:

• Before beginning your workout, put together a playlist of upbeat music featuring songs with faster tempos and positive lyrics.

• If you're having trouble relaxing, make a playlist on your computer of music that's a little bit calmer and slower, and call it the "chill out" playlist.

It is highly advised that you listen to binaural beats or isochronic tones, both of which create fluctuations in the activity of brain waves.

You might want to try playing some relaxing classical music in the background as you work on your task to improve your ability to focus.

Singing out loud while listening to some of your favorite uplifting tunes is a great way to lift your spirits.

Attending live performances allows one to feel the vibrations of the music firsthand and is highly recommended.

• If you want to increase your ability to concentrate, taking up an instrument, which can also serve as a type of meditation, is a good idea.

• Host a dance party with the express intention of having fun with your loved ones, whether that be your children, your friends, or your family.

• Include music in either your morning or evening routine and you'll be able to set the tone for the rest of the day.

• While you bathe in a warm bath, softly play some music that will calm and relax you in the background.

• If you want to really submerge yourself in the subject matter, make a weekly appointment with yourself during which you won't be doing anything else except listening to the audio.

• Listening to cheerful music that gets you pumped up before potentially nerve-wracking activities is a great way to ease your nerves.

• Include some music that has a relaxing effect on you when you practice yoga, meditation, or visualizing.

• Produce original personalized mixes that are an accurate representation of your individual musical personality.

• Be open to trying out various types of music; you never know when you might stumble into some new favorites that way.

Despite the fact that we have access to a vast library of music, the majority of the time it is simply playing in the background. Put in the effort to listen attentively and do so with the objective of consciously tapping into the power of what you are hearing. You've come to the right place to find the song that perfectly captures your mood.

Confronting The Facts And Occurrences Of The World

Interacting with others in real-life social contexts is frequently cited as one of the most challenging obstacles confronted by those who suffer from social anxiety, which is one of the most common types of anxiety. However, if you take the proper measures and make adequate preparations, you may gradually build up your tolerance for and confidence in these circumstances. These scenarios have the potential to create major anxiety; however, if you take the appropriate precautions and make adequate preparations, you can avoid feeling anxious. Those who struggle with social anxiety often find themselves in a number of difficult situations simply going about their daily lives. In this section, we will go over a variety of strategies that can be used to conquer these obstacles.

1. Coping Strategies for Employees Who Suffer from Social Anxiety at Work:

Suggestions for Those Who Give Presentations: Speaking in front of other people may be an extremely nerve-wracking experience, even for people who don't generally have problems with social anxiety. In order to find a solution to this problem, take the following advice into consideration:

The labor involved in preparation: Check to see that your speech or presentation has been thoroughly prepared. Building your self-confidence via regular practice is the most effective method.

Methods for both Taking In and Letting Out Air: You can ease your nerves and focus better by practicing deep breathing techniques both prior to and while you are giving your presentation.

You can encourage yourself by visualizing yourself effectively presenting a presentation, and then using this mental image. Research has demonstrated that engaging in activities that include visualization might help reduce anxiety and boost performance.

Techniques for the Formation of Networks: Doing the following will help you develop a more positive attitude toward networking, which is an important professional ability to have:

The Process of Establishing Objectives Establish networking goals that are both attainable and worthwhile before attending an event. You need to choose either the number of persons you will speak with or the subjects that will be discussed in the discussions that you will have.

Body Language It is essential to always have an open and confident body language no matter what the situation may be. When you are welcoming someone, you should always remember to smile and give them a firm handshake.

It will be much simpler to start and continue conversations if you prepare a list of open-ended questions to ask other people, so spend some time now compiling a list of such questions to use in future interactions.

How to Handle Social Events While You're at Work: Work-related social obligations can be challenging, but the following strategies can help you make the most of these opportunities:

Get there early. If you arrive early, you will have the chance to ease into the event as it gets started, which will make it much easier for you to interact with your coworkers gradually.

Find a Solution That Satisfies Everyone: You can start a conversation with your coworkers if you look for work-related topics that you both have an interest in or shared hobbies that you both enjoy.

Experimenting with active listening is something you should do because it involves paying attention to what other people are saying and demonstrating interest in what they have to say.

2. How to Overcome Social Anxiety When You're in a Social Setting: How to Handle Social Events, Including Parties and Gatherings:

Exposure to Gradual Changes: It is advisable to begin by attending meetings that are more intimate and on the more modest side of the spectrum before progressing to larger events.

Bringing a friend along: It is a good idea to bring a friend or a familiar face with you to the event if you want to have a more positive experience overall.

Put Your Attention On Other People Try talking to other people about their lives and showing a genuine interest in what they have to say rather than fixating on your own concerns all the time. This will help you avoid being preoccupied with your own problems.

Relationships and Dating: The World of Online Dating When it comes to starting conversations and getting to know potential partners before actually meeting in person, using online dating platforms can be a low-pressure way to do it.

Keep the lines of communication with your date open and honest about the challenges you face dealing with social anxiety. It is beneficial to both reduce stress and boost comprehension to talk about how you are feeling because it helps lessen tension.

Picking Locations That Offer a Satisfying Level of Coziness: You should go on dates at places where you will be the most comfortable, such as parks or cafes with low noise levels. This will ensure that you have a good time.

It is essential to make a proper introduction whenever you are in the company of new people: Even in situations that would be considered somewhat insignificant in terms of social interaction, such as beginning a new class or joining a new group, you should make it a point to introduce yourself to the other members.

Look for things that you have in common. Finding common ground with other individuals can be accomplished by looking for interests or hobbies that they all have in common with one another.

Active listening is a skill that can be honed by demonstrating a genuine interest in other people by intently listening to their tales and asking more questions about them. This type of listening may be practiced by displaying genuine interest in other people.

It is important to keep in mind that finding solutions to the problems that arise in real life is a process that requires time. Be patient with yourself, acknowledge that mistakes are an inevitable part of the learning process, and give yourself credit for even the tiniest of your successes. If you make a commitment to frequent practice and put the coping skills you've learnt to use, you'll find that your level of ease and self-assurance can progressively improve in a number of different social circumstances.

Exercising, getting a enough amount of sleep, and eating healthily are all aspects of self-care that are important to consider.

Take a seat somewhere that is comfortable, because we are going to talk about how a moderate amount of physical exercise, a sufficient amount of quality sleep, and a pinch of good eating can be some of your best allies in the fight against anxiety and depression.

Exert yourself.

In addition to being a helpful ally in the fight against emotional issues, physical activity is also an essential component of the exercises themselves and plays an important part in both of these. Endorphins are a type of feel-good hormone that are created in the brain as a result of physical activity. They are the ones who are in charge of putting a smile on your face and serving as the hype team for your disposition.

To participate, you do not need to be an athlete because any movement that you do will count toward the competition. Exercising is a mental and spiritual journey that can take many different forms, from dancing to your favorite songs to practicing yoga in your pajamas. The presence of nature adds an extra dimension to happiness and fosters the development of a mental playground. It is good for one's mental health to engage in activities that take place outside, where they can benefit from the sunshine and fresh air.

Exercising on a consistent basis is analogous to ingesting an energy tonic that boosts one's self-assurance and happiness. In order to accomplish this, it raises the levels of certain chemicals in the brain, such as serotonin and norepinephrine. This, in turn, results in an improvement in mood and a reduction in stress levels. Start with the smallest steps possible, make sure to recognize and appreciate your progress along the way, and do your best not to compare your development to that of fitness models. Increase the amount of movement you get during the day by doing things like walking further, taking the stairs instead of the elevator, or dancing as you clean. When it comes to obtaining mental well-being, every step you take brings you closer to progress, not perfection.

Exercising, which helps to improve mental health, can make your active trip feel more energizing and give you more control over the situation. Recognize that you are not perfect, focus your energy on improving yourself, and always bear in mind that each step you take puts you one step closer to obtaining mental contentment.

Fall asleep

Let's focus on one of the most significant parts of practicing good self-care: obtaining adequate sleep. Imagine it as the companion that helps you push anxiety and despair to the curb and get your life back on track. Imagine it as the sidekick to your superhero, Batman. Consider it to be your trusty sidekick. Imagine that when you don't get enough sleep, your brain takes on the demeanor of a sulky toddler who is having a severe temper tantrum. This is what your brain would look like. It's as if a drama queen has taken control of the situation, amplifying the significance of every minor setback so that it feels like a major catastrophe when in reality it's not even that bad.

Have you ever stayed up all night to finish a project, only to feel like a zombie when you got up the next morning? This is your brain's way of trying to tell you that it doesn't approve of what you're doing. Not getting enough sleep can result in more than just yawns and bloodshot eyes; it can also cause your mood to wildly fluctuate from one extreme to another. Just for a moment, picture yourself as having a shorter fuse, being more quickly irritated, and perhaps experiencing a little forgetfulness. A lack of sleep may increase a person's risk of developing anxiety disorders as well as depression, according to research that was published in Cox and 2022. This finding was made public.

Since this is your own personal fantasy movie, it doesn't matter if you're cruising through the clouds or if you're having a get-together with some pandas. Both scenarios are equally plausible. The following are some suggestions that will assist you in getting the most out of your time spent sleeping in order for you to awaken feeling revitalized:

Establish the mood by making the surrounding environment conducive to restful sleep. Imagine your bedroom as a peaceful haven; soft bedding, low lighting, and even just a hint of the scent of lavender can do wonders for creating this atmosphere.

Turn off electronic devices and put them away at least one hour before going to bed. It's possible that your smartphone and laptop are the ones keeping you awake at night. Instead, try reading a book, taking a relaxing warm bath, or doing some light stretching exercises.

Rituals performed before bedtime: Create calming bedtime rituals for yourself. Consuming herbal tea, engaging in activities that promote relaxation, or writing in a journal can help ease your mind into a state more conducive to sleep.

- Keeping To A Timetable That Is Consistent: Your Body Needs Routine In Order To Function Properly. Even On The Weekends, You Should Make An Effort To Stick To The Same Pattern Of Wakefulness And Sleep. This Helps To Regulate The Natural Clock Of Your Body So That You Can Get Adequate Rest.
- Caffeine And Heavy Meals Should Not Be Consumed In The Hours Leading Up To Bedtime. Pay Attention To Your Nutrition And Avoid Eating Meals That Are Too Large. If You Feel Hunger Coming On, Consider A Food That Is Easy To Digest.
- Transfer It: The Benefits Of Keeping Up With A Consistent Workout Regimen Can Be Compared To That Of Having A Superhero In Your Sleep. Just Keep In Mind That You Should Schedule Your Workout For The Early Part Of The Day So That Your Body Has Plenty Of Time To Wind Down Afterward Once You've Completed It.

Reduce Your Levels Of Stress By: Your Mind Might Turn Into A Worry Machine While You're Trying To Get Some Shut-Eye. You Might Try Practicing Mindfulness Meditation Or Deep Breathing Exercises To Silence The Wild Chatter That's Going On Within Your Head.

Bear In Mind That Sleep Is Always And Forever The Best Buddy That Your Mood Could Ask For. It's Like Hitting The Reset Button For Your Mind, So That You Can Face The Difficulties Of The Day Feeling Revitalized And Prepared To Take On Anything The World Might Throw At You.

Taking Responsibility For Your Path To Achieving Inner Calm

It is crucial to recognize that the path you travel from anxious to calm is unique to you if you are going to have any chance of making it through the journey from anxious to calm. In this chapter, we will take a look at the three primary characteristics that will lead you to a life of peace. Each of these factors is essential if you want to live a peaceful existence. In addition, we will talk about the inspiring experiences of regular individuals who have triumphed over their anxiety and found peace in their lives.

Putting in Place for the Future Objectives That Can Actually Be Achieved

The creation of appropriate goals for one's own personal growth is the first thing that should be done in the pursuit of mental tranquility. It is simple to let one's craving for instant gratification take control of one's life, but it is essential to keep in mind that change is a procedure that takes place over the course of time. Define milestones that are within your reach by taking into account the circumstances in which you find yourself as well as your present skills. Begin with little actions that can be accomplished with relative ease. These objectives may consist of anything as straightforward as practicing deep breathing methods for a few minutes on a daily basis or progressively exposing oneself to the things that make one anxious. Alternatively, these objectives may involve a combination of the two. If you make your objectives attainable and practical, you'll be able to keep yourself motivated and keep track of your progress at the same time.

Maintaining Vigilance over the Recurring Cycles of Your Anxiety

If you want to find your way through the emotional wasteland, gaining an awareness of the patterns of your anxiety is analogous to having a map in your possession. You should keep a notebook in which you record your experiences as well as your thoughts. Keep a log of the times you have anxiety, the circumstances that contribute to it, and how it affects you physically and emotionally, as well as the occasions when you experience anxiety. If you are able to recognize these patterns and follow them, you will be able to acquire insight into the underlying reasons for your anxiety and the ability to construct specific strategies to manage them. If you are able to do this, you will also be able to build specific methods to manage them. You will notice changes and patterns over the course of time that are representative of your degree of achievement. These changes and patterns will become apparent to you. Keeping a log of the patterns of your anxiety can be a beneficial way for both finding out more about yourself and getting better at improving yourself.

One ought to make a big deal out of the victories that are relatively insignificant.

It is vital to appreciate and take delight in the journey's many modest wins along the road in order to pursue tranquility. These victories can be found along the way. Every victory that may be claimed in this endeavor represents a victory over anxiety. Recognize and honor your accomplishments, whether it's making it through the day without feeling anxious, successfully applying a relaxation strategy while coping with a stressful scenario, or accomplishing a goal you've set for yourself. If you take the time to appreciate these victories, however obviously tiny they may seem, you may be able to promote healthy behaviors and build your confidence in your capacity to effectively regulate anxiety.

True Stories Of The Struggles And Triumphs Against Anxiety Experienced By Regular People In Everyday Life.

Let's have a look at the experiences of regular individuals who have battled and won against the challenges they've faced so that we can provide you with further motivation and inspiration. These individuals are familiar with the concerns and apprehensions that you are now feeling since they have been there before.

Their experiences demonstrate that one is able to win the battle against anxiety and that one can arrive to a place of peace in one's life. On their journey from nervous to calm, each person's tale illustrates a different tactic or method that has been useful to them in achieving this goal. Their stories will motivate you to keep going on your journey toward a life that is less chaotic and has more of an impact on who you are as an individual.

Bear in mind that the process of getting from anxious to calm is going to be different for everyone, and there is no one approach that is going to work for everyone. Instead, you should keep in mind that there is no one way that will work for everyone. You will be well-equipped to walk this path with perseverance and determination if you set acceptable goals for yourself, pay attention to the patterns of anxiety that you encounter, enjoy your successes, and draw encouragement from the accomplishments of others. enjoy your successes and draw motivation from the accomplishments of others. If you set your mind to it, you can find peace, and the journey of a lifetime that you've planned for yourself is the key to getting you there.

Keeping Hold of Something While Also Letting It Go

When addressing anxiety, the phrases "embracing" and "releasing" take on a considerable relevance because they reflect the delicate balance that people who suffer from anxiety often try to attain in their day-to-day lives. This is why the phrases take on a significant relevance when discussing anxiety.

Accepting the presence of worry, often known as "embracing" it, is preferable to denying or seeking to suppress it in any other way. It is necessary to recognize that anxiety, like any other feeling, is a normal and natural component of the human experience. This fact should not be ignored. Individuals who embrace their anxiety allow themselves to address it head-on, realizing that it is not a show of weakness but rather a natural response to the many stressors and uncertainties in their surroundings. This helps these individuals realize that embracing their anxiety is not a sign of weakness but rather a natural response.

Despite this, there is a common misconception that "embracing" anxiety means giving in to its dominance over one's life. Instead, it is an act of self-compassion, a way of saying, "I acknowledge that I'm feeling anxious, and that's okay." Because it reduces the amount of internal conflict and self-criticism that commonly accompany anxiety, this recognition can be an effective first step in controlling the condition. Recognizing the existence of an anxiety disorder and accepting it as a part of your life can be an effective first step in controlling anxiety.

A further requirement for "embracing" anxiety is an understanding of the patterns and triggers that are connected with it. People can begin to obtain a better knowledge of the circumstances, ideas, or feelings that tend to make their anxiety worse by working on developing their self-awareness and possibly seeking the advice of a therapist. This can help people start to get a better handle on the circumstances, ideas, or feelings that tend to make their anxiety worse. This comprehension lays the framework for the development of successful coping mechanisms that are customized to the specific needs of the individual and provides a platform for carrying out such development.

"Releasing" one's anxiousness is the antithesis of preserving this precarious equilibrium, which is the goal of keeping this equilibrium. It is about breaking free from the grip that worrying may have, not only on a person's thoughts but also on their actual body. When anxiety reaches a crippling level, it can kick off a chain reaction of physical and psychological symptoms, such as a racing heart rate, racing thoughts, and a sensation of impending doom. When anxiety reaches this level, it can be extremely difficult to function normally.

"Releasing" anxiety is finding techniques to minimize the symptoms of worry and reestablish a sense of tranquility and control over the situation. "Releasing" anxiety also refers to the act of "letting go" of anxiety. This can be accomplished by the practice of a variety of different relaxation techniques, such as exercises that focus on deep breathing, progressive muscular relaxation, or mindfulness meditation, among other practices. These practices provide people the option to take a step back from the intensity of their anxiety, so providing a space in which they are able to regain perspective and a sense of stability. They also allow people the opportunity to take a step back from the intensity of their worry.

In addition, "releasing" anxiety often requires setting boundaries for worrying and ruminating about the issue at hand. Anxiety has a tendency of taking control of our brain and leading us down never-ending rabbit holes of "what ifs" and worst-case situations. This can make us feel helpless and exacerbate the problem. Individuals might be able to liberate themselves from this effect on them by setting out specific times in their calendars for worrying and only allowing themselves to think anxious thoughts during those times. This tactic helps prevent anxiety from taking over a person's mental landscape and making it harder for them to function in their day-to-day existence by preventing it from occurring in the first place.

Receiving encouragement from other people is another important component that is crucial to "releasing" worry. Talking to a therapist or counselor can provide a safe and non-judgmental atmosphere in which to communicate anxious thoughts and to receive help on how to properly control them. This can be beneficial for people who want to learn how to better manage their anxiety. Support from friends and family members is also a crucial component in the process of conquering anxiety. This is due to the fact that emotional comfort and a sense of belonging can be brought about through social ties.

The intricate journey that people who battle with anxiety go on can be reflected in the delicate balance that needs to be struck between "embracing" and "releasing" their concern. The journey that these people go on can be thought of as a series of nuanced steps. The most important thing is to recognize that worry is present without giving in to it or letting it control any aspect of one's life in any way. People can recover a sense of control over their lives and resiliency if they learn to embrace their anxiety with self-compassion, acquire insight into the triggers that produce it, and create strategies to cope with it. If people learn to accept their anxiety with self-compassion, they are more likely to be resilient.

When people learn methods to lessen the immediate hold that worry has on them, they are better equipped to ride the turbulent waves of anxiety with greater grace and composure. The process of overcoming anxiety must begin with this step, as it is one of the most important steps. A person's capability to regain their equilibrium and embrace a life that is not defined by worry but is enhanced by their ability to control it can be improved through the process of releasing anxiety, which offers them this skill. This can be accomplished by the utilization of strategies for relaxation, the establishment of boundaries with regard to anxiety, or the solicitation of aid from other people.

A Concise Guide to Relaxing Nights, as well as a Better Understanding of the Anxiety That Comes With Not Being Able to Sleep

What Precisely Is Meant By The Term "Sleep Anxiety"?

Sleep Is Essential Necessary If You Want To Keep Both Your Physical And Emotional Wellbeing In Good Shape. On The Other Side, The Very Idea Of Going To Bed Might Be Enough To Trigger An Overwhelming Amount Of Anxiety In Some People, Which Can Lead To Problems Falling Asleep Or Staying Asleep During The Night. This Can Make It Difficult To Get To Sleep Or Stay Asleep. This Condition Is Commonly Referred To As Sleep Anxiety; However, It Is Also Sometimes Called Somniphobia Or Sleep-Related Anxiety Disorder.

The Outward And Internal Manifestations Of Anxiety When One Is Asleep

If You Suffer From Sleep Anxiety, You May Experience A Number Of Symptoms. These Symptoms Can Have A Significant Influence On The Quality Of Your Sleep As Well As Your Ability To Operate Properly Throughout The

Day. If You Want To Improve Your Ability To Sleep And Your Ability To Function Normally During The Day, You Should Address Your Sleep Anxiety. The Following Are Some Of The Possible Manifestations Of These Symptoms:

If You Are Having Difficulties Falling Asleep, You May Find That It Is Tough For You To Relax And Put Your Thoughts On Hold, Which Keeps You From Going Asleep At Night. If This Is The Case, You May Find That It Is Difficult To Put Your Ideas On Pause.

Restlessness: Even If You Are Able To Fall Asleep, You May Discover That You Wake Up Multiple Times Throughout The Night Feeling Restless And Unable To Find A Position That Is Comfortable For You. This May Be The Case Even If You Are Able To Get To Sleep.

If Your Mind Is Filled With Racing Thoughts, Anxieties, Or Fears While You Try To Fall Asleep, It May Be Difficult For You To Quiet Your Mind And Concentrate On Falling Asleep. If This Is The Case, You May Find It Difficult To Fall Asleep.

Anxiety Over Falling Asleep Or Staying Asleep Can Manifest Itself In A Variety Of Physical Ways, Including An Increased Heart Rate, Profuse Sweating, Tense Muscles, And An Overall Sense Of Unease. Among The Other Physical Signs Is An Apprehensive Or Uncomfortable Feeling.

Constant Weariness Throughout The Day Because Of The Disruptions In Your Normal Sleep Pattern, It Is Conceivable That You Could Experience Excessive Daytime Sleepiness, Feelings Of Tiredness, And Difficulty Concentrating.

Help Your Child Overcome Their Social Anxiety By Giving Them Your Support.

Rachel, a young woman who lived in the suburbs, was a resident of a peaceful community that was nestled away in a corner. Despite possessing a lot of intelligence and ingenuity, she suffered with the ever-feared enemy that is known as social anxiety. She started each new school day with the looming specter of having to interact with her students, which sparked a seething mix of fear and anxiety within her. She was terrified of having to interact with her classmates.

Rachel's parents, being acute observers of their daughter's emotional storm, came to the realization that they needed to assist their daughter on this hero's quest to battle the monsters that were within her. They embarked on a quest to locate some kind of holy grail that may point them in the right path so that they could assist Rachel in the heroic effort that she was making.

Their virtuous journey began with real heart-to-heart dialogues, during which they bestowed upon Rachel the priceless gift of an open ear and a sanctuary free from judgment for her ideas and emotions. This occurred while they were on their vacation. This marked the start of the adventure for them. This thoughtful deed provided as a soothing ointment, which assisted in calming the rough seas of her stress.

They came to the conclusion that exposure therapy would be the best method to help them reach their objective. Rachel was gradually put in awkward social circumstances as a part of this process. These were the precise kinds of situations that used to make her apprehensive. They began with pretty meaningless endeavors, such as bringing a close friend over for a game session they could both participate in. They started becoming involved in social antics that were increasingly dangerous and sophisticated as Rachel's level of boldness increased.

The parents of Rachel were very adept at using all of the different instruments that were provided in the social skill development session. They were proficient in the art of discourse, developed their abilities in the time-honored art of meticulous listening, and perfected the magic of maintaining consistent eye contact throughout the conversation. They made these weighty issues into amusing games, and as a result, the scary realm of social interaction became more accessible.

The idea that one should pursue one's goals in a manner that is in line with one's capabilities emerged as their guiding principle. Rachel and her parental mentors collaborated on the development of a set of attainable objectives, a progression of steps that included participating in classroom dialogue and joining student organizations at her school. Rachel's self-assurance arose like a phoenix from the ashes after each win, putting an end to the raging dragon that was her social anxiety.

As the tides of time moved back and forth, Rachel went through a metamorphosis that was nothing short of incredible to witness. At first, the thought of facing the school day filled me with dread, but over time, that dread morphed into an eager anticipation of expanding my horizons intellectually and socially. As the change of their daughter into a delightful and outgoing young explorer took place in front of her parents' eyes, it caused them joy to watch the process develop.

Rachel, equipped with the information that she had acquired on her journey, continued to put these laudable practices into action. Her social anxiety, which used to be a powerful adversary, has significantly decreased to the point where it is scarcely audible now. Despite the initial difficulties that everyone had to deal with, she stood victorious, a beacon of hope for everyone, and a living demonstration of the boundless potential that resided inside every soul. She was living proof that every single person have the capacity to accomplish everything they set their mind to.

Contribution to the Decision-Making Process

Understanding the cognitive triangle not only equips one with a set of practical tools that facilitates the making of well-informed decisions, but it also raises one's overall degree of self-awareness. Almost never does one person make a decision on their own, regardless of how major or inconsequential it may be. They emerge from the tangled web of previous ideas, emotions, and deeds that have come before them. By putting your attention on each of the cognitive triangle's vertices, you can achieve an unprecedented degree of clarity in the processes that underlie your decision-making. The decision you make about how to react in a particular situation is the product of a complex interaction between a number of different elements.

Decisions That Were Made After Much Contemplation

The process of making a decision often starts in an individual's thoughts, particularly when the individual is attempting to locate a solution to a problem or choose an alternative that is rational. Your perception of the numerous possibilities and the risks that are involved will be molded by the concepts that you give some attention to thinking about. For instance, if you're considering transferring jobs but are on the fence about whether or not to do so, telling yourself positive affirmations like "The new role offers better growth prospects" can help tip the scales in favor of making the move. Be aware, though, of cognitive fallacies such as "all-or-nothing" thinking that may cause you to incorrectly interpret the nature of the options that are open to you. This could lead to you making a decision that you later regret. It is of the utmost importance to put these initial presumptions to the test and explore them utilizing evidence and rational thought.

Decisions that are Influenced by Emotions and Feelings

Emotions have the potential to be substantial motivators in decision-making, both for the better and for the worse. This can be said for both positive and negative outcomes. When time or resources are limited, they frequently provide a shortcut to a conclusion, and in order to do so, they tap into your natural or learned instincts. Take, for example, the sense of dread in the setting of a dangerous scenario; it has the capacity to motivate you to take immediate action, skipping over the requirement for in-depth cerebral thought in the process. Even though this can be adaptive in specific contexts, actions that are inspired by emotions can be reckless and lack foresight if they are not checked. This is especially true if the emotions are strong. Before making a decision that could have significant repercussions, it is essential to conduct a "emotional audit" of yourself. This is a crucial phase in the process of "emotional auditing," which can be of great assistance in this scenario.

The Gathering Storm of Behavioural Changes

The choices that will be taken in the future will also be influenced by events that occurred in the past. Let's imagine that you've decided to make a commitment to a fitness program; the routine that you've formed of attending to the gym on a continuous basis can make it easier for you to say "no" to an unhealthy meal. It is also likely that the individual in issue has a history of engaging in avoidance or procrastination behaviors, both of which make it more challenging for the individual to make a choice that is productive. When you have this awareness, you will be able to disrupt maladaptive patterns of behavior by deliberately choosing activities that are in opposition to those patterns. This will allow you to change your behavior.

How the Triangle's Structure Operates

Consider the following real-world scenario: despite the fact that it gives you the willies just to think about it, you've decided to deliver a speech in front of an audience. When you combine the thought, "This could be good for my career," with an emotional audit that recognizes worry as well as anticipation, your behavior of replying "yes" becomes a holistic decision. This happens when you link the thinking that "This could be good for my career" with the emotional audit. It is the sum total of a constructive behavior, a balanced emotional state, and a positive state of thinking, each of which feeds into and off of the other.

The cognitive triangle gives you a framework that you may use to make decisions that are all-encompassing and that take into account a number of different factors. You can cultivate a method of decision-making that is more rational and well-informed by challenging the logic behind your thoughts, analyzing the appropriateness of your feelings, and taking into account the momentum of your prior actions.

When we claim that cognitive behavioral therapy (CBT) gives you the power to live a more purposeful life, this is exactly what we mean by that statement. It provides you with the ability to navigate the complex decision-making scenarios that life throws at you with greater nuance and knowledge, enabling you to shape your choices in a manner that is congruent with your long-term goals and values. The implications of making better decisions will have an impact that is incomprehensible throughout the course of a person's entire life. Because of this, the cognitive triangle is not just a tool for personal development; rather, it is also a tool for the betterment of interpersonal relationships and of society as a whole. They not only make your life better, but also the lives of the people with whom you come into touch.

Attempt To Retain Mastery Over Your Powerful Emotions

someone may already have cautioned you about how difficult going through puberty can be, and you may be familiar with the term "emotional rollercoaster" and may have even been on one yourself at some point in your life. Have you ever gone through a phase in which you were overjoyed beyond measure, only to be followed by another in which you were profoundly depressed? Have you ever experienced a sudden change in your disposition to the point that you were unable to make sense of it or discern between the numerous feelings that you were experiencing? If so, describe the event. Because of how common it is, you shouldn't let your concerns about it get the better of you. In order to start exerting some level of control over your emotions, the first thing you need to do is learn how to give each one a name. If you are unable to see the differences between them, you will be unable to successfully manage them. Studies have shown that infants, adults, and older individuals are better at identifying and labeling emotions than teenagers. However, these advantages are due to different variables, thus it is unclear why toddlers, adults, and older adults are better. Babies frequently just experience a single feeling at a time, which makes it easy for the baby as well as the individuals around them to comprehend how the baby is now feeling. Adults, on the other hand, have the ability to discern between the various emotions that they may feel all at once. Teenagers are in the middle of the emotional spectrum, which means that they are able to perceive a larger range of sentiments but are still unable to discern between them. This indicates that teenagers are in the middle of the emotional spectrum. As a direct consequence of this, they are also unable to exert proper control over them (McConchie, 2018).

It is essential to your entire physical and mental health, as well as to your level of success, that you learn how to exercise self-control over your moods and behaviors. If you are able to recognize the ideal times and techniques for expressing your sentiments, your relationships will be more robust, and you will have a better grasp of who you are. If you are able to explain how you feel, you will know the appropriate periods and methods. You will find that you have significantly higher levels of self-assurance, pleasure, and contentment as a direct result of your greater ability to regulate your feelings. When you have reached the point where you have perfected the ability to manage your feelings, you will be able to do so regardless of the circumstance or the emotion that you are currently experiencing. Regardless of how powerful they are, you will have the ability to handle dealing with them. It makes no difference regardless. This chapter will walk you through 15 activities, five of which will assist you in being more aware of your feelings, and ten of which will teach you how to correctly manage with those sensations.

(Continued) Strategies for the Handling of Stress and Anxiety Over the Long Term

Deliverance From the Consequences of Stress On a Permanent Basis

Imagine for a moment that you have access to a buffer that shields you from the effects of stress at all times, irrespective of the challenges that life presents you with. In this final piece, we are going to talk about the two most significant aspects of stress reduction that a person can practice during their entire life: Increasing your ability to bounce back from adversity and making your life less stressful. You will be able to handle the challenges that life throws at you with composure, and as a result, you will experience less worry as a result of your ability to understand these ideas and how to apply them.

Developing a Defense against Pressure and Strain

Having the mental and emotional fortitude to overcome hardship is analogous to having mental and emotional armor. This concept alludes to one's ability to pick oneself back up after being struck down by life's challenges. People who are resilient are similar to rubber balls; they can take a hit, but they always come back stronger than they were before.

The following are some of the ways that building resilience can be accomplished:

1. Optimism: Make it a point to always see the positive side of things and retrain your mind to do so, especially when you are confronted with difficult situations. Instead of dwelling on the errors of the past, you should look for the lessons to be learned and possibilities to make improvements.

2. Emotional Regulation: Figure out how to have an effective grasp on your feelings and learn how to effectively regulate them. This indicates that rather than allowing feelings of anger or despair to overtake you, you should explore for healthy ways to express those emotions and build techniques to manage with them. Specifically, you should look for ways to release anger through exercise or journaling.

3. Get social support by maintaining ties with people who are able to offer emotional support, such as friends and family members. Share with them your thoughts and feelings, and in return, always make yourself available to them whenever they have a question or concern.

4. Methods and Strategies for Solving Problems Reframing problems as opportunities for progress rather than insurmountable obstacles is one method that can be utilized in the process of finding solutions to problems. Convert these difficulties into a series of more manageable tasks, and then start to work figuring out the answers.

5. Engage in healthy self-care practices by engaging in regular physical activity, keeping a nutritious diet, and utilizing

relaxation strategies such as meditation. This will assist you in maintaining both your mental and physical health.

Imagine for a moment that you are terminated from your job, a circumstance that is incredibly stressful for anyone. To build resilience, you must first acknowledge that you are feeling sentiments of disappointment and fear, but you must also look at the circumstance as an opportunity to start over. Only then can you acquire the ability to bounce back from adversity. You might want to look into new employment opportunities, get your resume up to date, and network with people who can provide you with support and direction.

How To Preserve Your Own Internal Calm

Finding inner peace is a significant step on the way to overcoming fear, concern, and despair on the path to overcoming fear, worry, and despair. However, the capacity to maintain one's composure in the face of challenges encountered in life can be considered to be of equal importance. In this chapter, we will discuss tactics and techniques for maintaining your composure and making it a continuous travel companion. Keeping your composure is essential when traveling.

The First Is to Practice Mindfulness

Practice being present and alert throughout your day-to-day activities. Be fully present in every moment, whether you're doing a brief activity, having a conversation, or spending time in nature. Through the practice of mindfulness, you can learn to better control your stress, preserve your sense of center, and stay in touch with the peace that is inside you.

2. expressing thankfulness in a journal

Maintaining a journal of gratitude can serve as a regular reminder of everything that you have to be grateful for. Maintain a running list of all of your blessings, no matter how large or small. This practice fosters a more positive outlook on life and helps to keep a pleasant disposition.

3. Engaging in Regular Religious Practices

Maintain your spiritual discipline by praying regularly and having faith in what you believe. Make it an essential part of your daily routine so that you don't risk losing contact with the source of your power and wisdom and ensure that you do it every day.

4th in a series of self-care rituals

Make taking care of yourself a primary priority rather than just a strategy for the near term. Participate in pursuits that can revitalize your body, mind, and spirit, such as reading, making art, going for walks in the great outdoors, or simply spending time with the people you care about the most in this world.

5. Management of One's Emotions

Develop your capacity for emotional control and put it into practice if you want to be able to properly manage difficult feelings. You are able to regain emotional equilibrium by engaging in practices such as deep breathing, meditation, and visualization.

6. Define Your Boundaries

Always remember to set reasonable boundaries in the commitments and relationships you have. By establishing distinct limits for yourself, you can protect your mental health and take care of your overall well-being. 7. Seek the Advice of Professionals

Carry on your treatment or counseling sessions with the mental health professional you've been working with as needed. They may be able to provide you with useful tools and encouragement that can assist you in overcoming emotional difficulties and put your mind at ease.

8. Donate to those in need.

Regularly engage in acts of kindness and generosity toward others. Helping other people will not only make you joyful, but it will also help you feel more at peace with yourself and enhance your connection to a higher purpose.

9. Take Into Consideration Your Trip

Consider your journey at regular intervals and give it some thought. Recognize how far you've come and give yourself credit for all you've achieved, no matter how small. This self-reflection could prove to be a powerful reminder of the inner fortitude you possess.

10. Surround yourself with upbeat and positive individuals.

Positivity can be brought into one's environment through the reading of uplifting books, the company of encouraging individuals, or the possession of motivational goods. Create an environment that nourishes your spirit and helps you maintain a calm state of mind within yourself.

11. Adapt Yourself to Life's Constant Changes

The challenges that life presents will constantly be shifting. Embrace change by demonstrating both resilience and adaptability. Have faith in your talents to prevail despite the challenges you face while maintaining your inner composure.

12. Assuming Complete Command

You are able to keep your inner peace by releasing the need for excessive control over the situation. Recognize that not everything is in your control and that there are certain things that you must leave in the hands of a higher power. There are some things that you must leave in the hands of a higher power. Give up, and put your trust in the divine direction that will be provided.

13. Remain steadfast in your commitment to your faith.

Maintain a close connection to your religious practice. Continue your spiritual development by participating in worship services and activities that bolster your relationship to God, such as reading the Bible and praying.

14. Let go and be willing to forgive.

Learn to forgive yourself as well as others for the wrongs you've done in the past and the injuries you've caused. Keeping grudges against oneself and harboring self-blame is disruptive to one's inner peace. When you forgive, you free yourself from the burden that the past has placed upon you.

Keeping the peace within oneself requires consistent practice and mindful effort. Being focused and committed to achieving inner peace is one way to increase the likelihood that it will become a trustworthy companion. You will be able to face the challenges that life throws at you with elegance, fortitude, and a heart that is full of enduring tranquility as a result of this.

Getting rid of dread is the single most important step in reducing the effects of social anxiety.

Fear, which is one of the strongest and most fundamental feelings that humans experience, is at the root of social anxiety. Fear commonly paralyzes people in social circumstances and causes them to feel isolated as a result. In this extensive chapter, which is an essential part of effectively managing social anxiety, we discuss strategies and methods that are essential for conquering fear. This is a necessary stage in the process.

In Regards to Fear and Understanding Anxiety, Social Anxiety

The fear of obtaining a negative evaluation or judgment from other people is at the heart of social anxiety. This worry incorporates a number of other concerns as well, including the following:

- The worry of Rejection: This refers to the anxiety that comes with the worry of being rejected or left out of social gatherings. - The Fear of Being Left Out: This refers to the fear of being left out of social events.

This anxiety arises from the worry of saying or acting in a manner that others could find embarrassing or dumb, establishing a pervasive fear of being humiliated as a result. - fear of Embarrassment: This anxiety stems from the worry of saying or acting in a way that others could find embarrassing or dumb.

Fear of Attention: This creates greater self-consciousness and manifests as discomfort or anxiety when one is the center of attention, such as in public speaking or group debates. - Social Anxiety Disorder: This is characterized by an extreme avoidance of social situations that put one in the spotlight.

- Anxiety Regarding Criticism This disorder involves an aversion to criticism, mocking, or rejection from peers, which results in an ongoing concern that one is being judged in an unfavorable manner.

Techniques for Overcoming Fear in the Context of Social Anxiety

The first step is cognitive remodeling.

Cognitive restructuring is a core method for treating anxiety and fear. This strategy entails identifying and challenging irrational or pessimistic thinking in order to alleviate anxiety and fear. the stages that are as follows:

- Acknowledge the presence of unpleasant thoughts: Pay close attention to the way that you think when you're with other people. Do they have an unrealistically negative outlook on life or are they overly critical of themselves?

- Problematical Concepts and Ideas: Analyze the premises upon which these notions are based to ascertain whether or not they are backed by true data or whether or not they are the consequence of skewed perspectives. Instead of holding opinions that are incorrect, try adopting some that are more logical and practical.

- Practice having compassion for yourself. You should show yourself the same amount of compassion and understanding that you would give to a dear friend. Recognize that you are not alone in making mistakes and occasionally experiencing anxiety when interacting with others.

Embracing the Darkness as We Wind Our Way Through the Labyrinths of Anxiety

Women frequently find themselves caught up in the intricate web of cultural standards, expectations, and roles in the fabric of life, with each thread producing a pattern of stress and anxiety in their lives. It takes a group of women to successfully navigate the complex terrain of worry; during their search for relief, they frequently take the same turns and travel the same highways. The first step on this journey, which will shed light on the paths leading to recovery and equilibrium, is coming to a knowledge of the many manifestations of concern. In this chapter, we will investigate the many different terrains of anxiety, becoming familiar with their characteristics and learning how to navigate our way through them.

The Many Differing Forms That Anxiety Can Take

Anxiety can manifest itself in a wide variety of guises, each of which has its own set of echoes and shadows. The following is a list of symptoms that are frequently associated with anxiety:

Generalized anxiety disorder is abbreviated as GAD. GAD casts a pall over many elements of life, including relationships and employment, by spreading unceasing rumors of anxiety and concern. This spreads a shadow over many aspects of life. It is constantly there, carrying with it the bodily echoes of strain and tiredness even when everything appears to be at rest.

This type of anxiety expresses itself as an abrupt storm of terror and panic, which is then followed by a frenetic heartbeat and a rush of breath. Panic disorder is commonly triggered by being in a crowded place or being in the spotlight when giving a presentation.

Anxiety Disorder Related to Social Interactions: Avoiding social situations causes social anxiety, which manifests itself as a persistent feeling of unease and a persistent fear of being judged or embarrassed in front of other people.

Obsessive-Compulsive Disorder (OCD): OCD is a dance of activities that is performed to hush the whispering of anxiety, even when the dance seems senseless. Intrusive thoughts and the need to perform routines are at the root of obsessive-compulsive disorder (OCD).

Post-Traumatic Stress Disorder (PTSD): PTSD is the emotional whirlwind that is brought on by the echoes of the past, the flashback of nightmares, and the shadow of previous disasters.

Two separate chapters

What signs point to the presence of an anxiety disorder?

Because everyone experiences some level of anxiety, it is impossible to determine when those feelings might become something more serious like an anxiety disorder.

If your feelings of concern and dread start to have a debilitating effect on you over time, you should seek the advice of a mental health expert so that you can get some relief from them. Anxiety disorders can take on a wide variety of guises; the following, however, are some of the most frequently encountered symptoms:

The pace of heartbeat and breathing quickens; muscles tense up; there is a tightening in the chest; rising anxieties that are unjustified are accompanied with restlessness; and the chest feels as though it is getting tighter. Developing an obsession for something that isn't important will lead to obsessive conduct.

If you have a friend or family member who displays these symptoms, you should have a conversation with them about the likely issue they are dealing with and suggest that they speak with a mental health expert.

Why do people suffer from anxiety disorders?

The following are the most common causes that contribute to the development of anxiety disorders:

Histories in the patient's family It's possible that people who struggle with anxiety concerns on a regular basis have a history of mental health problems in their families.

For example, OCD may be passed down from parent to child.

Things that can make you anxious are: Stressful conditions, including having to work long hours or dealing with the death of a loved one, can also trigger the onset of anxiety symptoms.

Problems with one's health: Certain medical disorders, such as thyroid problems, asthma, diabetes, or heart problems, can also bring on feelings of anxiety.

Patients who suffer from depression are at an increased risk for developing signs of anxiety disorders.

For instance, a someone who has struggled with depression for a significant amount of time may start to perform poorly in their professional life.

Because of this, there may be increased strain at work, which may lead to feelings of worry.

When the effects of alcohol, drugs, or other substances begin to wear off (known medically as "withdrawal"), heavy users of these substances are more likely to have anxiety disorders.

characteristics of one's mind: People who have particular personality qualities, such as a need for control or a tendency toward perfectionism, are more likely to experience episodes of anxiety-related disorders.

Different types of anxiety disorders

Anxiety has a variety of effects on different people, which might direct them to experience a wide range of difficulties. The following categories of anxiety disorders account for the vast majority of cases:

The condition known as generalized anxiety disorder (GAD) Patients diagnosed with GAD suffer from severe anxiety and worry about a variety of different scenarios and occurrences.

They have a difficult time keeping their anxiety, concern, and restlessness under control, which is accompanied by a persistent "feeling of being revved up or on edge." These individuals' worry is unreasonable given that there is no identifiable explanation for it in their lives.

Obsessive Compulsive Disorder (OCD) is an abbreviation for this condition. Patients who suffer from OCD are plagued by persistent anxious thoughts and thoughts that are upsetting.

They find that doing particular chores over and over again helps them feel less anxious.

For instance, a person who has a fear of polluted environments and germs might wash their hands and the things in their home on a regular basis.

It is possible to conquer challenges related to anxiety, but doing so requires one to refrain from underestimating the gravity of the situation.

If you suffer any of the symptoms described above, it is strongly recommended that you seek the advice and treatment of a qualified medical expert as soon as possible. Treatment for anxiety disorders may involve anti-anxiety medication, counseling, or a combination of the two approaches.

Improving Both Physical And Emotional Intimacy With The Help Of Direction

Although attention deficit hyperactivity disorder (ADHD) can make dating more challenging, there are some activities and strategies that people who are in relationships with someone who has ADHD can implement into their daily routine to strengthen their mental and physical intimacy. These activities have the potential to assist in the consolidation of connections between couples, the lowering of barriers to communication, and the raising of levels of mutual comprehension.

1. Strengthening the Emotional Bonds Between Us

1. Expressive Writing: In order to enable one another to freely communicate their experiences, ideas, and feelings, encourage one another to participate in creative writing activities. People may find it easier to

understand the problems and thoughts of one another as a result of this.

2. The "Emotional Check-In" Procedure : A mental check-in should take place at a predetermined period, preferably on a daily basis. During this time period, each participant has the opportunity to share their thoughts and the events they go through on a daily basis, which promotes empathy and comprehension.

3. Make it a habit to express thankfulness and appreciation to one another Do your best to make it a habit to express gratitude and appreciation to one another on a regular basis. By acknowledging and praising one another for their efforts and talents, emotional connection can be strengthened between people.

2. Facilitating Productive Interpersonal Communication

1. Engage in exercises of active listening, in which one person speaks while the other person pays attentive attention to what is being said without interrupting. After that, you should look for new employment. This

encourages attentive listening as well as hearing with compassion.

2. Prearranged Forms of Communication Time: Assign particular times throughout the day for having important conversations when there will be few interruptions. Address your fears, talk about what you have planned, and be open and honest about what you have experienced over this time.

3. Words Beginning with "I Feel" Encourage non-confrontational communication and reduce the likelihood of misunderstandings by recommending the use of phrases beginning with "I feel" when expressing feelings and worries.

3. Developing a Closer Physical Relationship

1. The exercise of mindful touch consists of having partners take turns caressing each other while focusing on their sensations and the nature of their relationship. This helps to cultivate awareness and focus during one's free time. 2. Activities That Build Relationships: Participate in activities that enhance physical closeness through coordinated movement, such

as partner yoga, dancing, or cooking. These kinds of exercises have the potential to foster physical bonding as well as teamwork.

3. Conducting research Activities that engage the senses: Participate with the rest of the group in a range of activities that engage the senses, such as creating food and savoring the flavors or going for a walk in the woods to take in the sights and sounds. As a consequence of this, there may be an increase in physical proximity.

Without a question, intimacy and the bonds that bind relationships are put to the test in special ways by ADHD. The first step in overcoming these obstacles is gaining an understanding of them, in both their mental and their bodily manifestations.

By putting into practice effective communication strategies, cultivating emotional intimacy through expressive practices, and fostering physical closeness through mindful touch and shared activities, couples can navigate the complexities of ADHD and create a relationship that thrives on genuine intimacy and connection.

Patience, understanding, and concerted effort on both partners' parts are required in order for couples to triumph over the challenges posed by ADHD.

Prescription medications and alternative or complementary treatments

There is a wide variety of treatment options available for anxiety, such as medication and other types of talk therapy. The individual's specific needs, preferences, and the severity of their anxiety will guide the selection of an appropriate form of treatment. Let's investigate both conventional and alternative methods of treatment in great detail:

Medications Used to Treat Anxiety:

Medication Used in the Treatment of Anxiety

Benzodiazepines are medications that have a rapid onset of action and provide immediate relief from the symptoms of anxiety. However, because of the risk of becoming dependent on them and experiencing withdrawal symptoms, they are often only recommended for use in the short term.

Buspirone is a non-benzodiazepine medication that may be purchased without a prescription and is used to treat generalized anxiety disorder (GAD). There is a reduced possibility of dependency.

Antidepressants are characterized by:

- Selective serotonin reuptake inhibitors, or SSRIs: Medications like fluoxetine (Prozac), sertraline (Zoloft), and escitalopram (Lexapro) belong to this category. They are widely recommended for the treatment of anxiety disorders such generalized anxiety disorder (GAD), social anxiety disorder, and panic disorder.

- SNRIs, or serotonin-norepinephrine reuptake inhibitors, are a class of medications used to treat anxiety disorders. These medications include venlafaxine (Effexor) and duloxetine (Cymbalta).

- Tricyclic antidepressants (TCAs) and monoamine oxidase inhibitors (MAOIs): Despite the fact that these older antidepressants have a greater number of adverse effects and dietary restrictions, they may be utilized in cases when other treatments are ineffective.

Beta-Blockers: Occasionally, the physical signs and symptoms of anxiety, such as trembling and a rapid heartbeat, can be treated with beta-blockers like propranolol, which are in the class of medications known as beta-blockers. They are commonly used as a treatment for social anxiety as well as performance anxiety.

Medication used in the treatment of anxiety includes:

Medication and talk therapy, such as cognitive-behavioral therapy (also known as CBT), are frequently used together as part of an integrative strategy for the management of anxiety.

- Medication should never be given without the supervision of a trained medical practitioner since there is a possibility that it could have unintended effects and that the dosage will need to be adjusted carefully.

Alternate Approaches to the Treatment of Anxiety:

Counseling: therapy

Cognitive-behavioral therapy (often known as CBT), exposure therapy, and mindfulness-based therapies are all effective treatments for anxiety that do not need the use of pharmaceuticals.

The Struggle With Anxiety And How Mindfulness Can Help

It is necessary for each individual to devise their own method of incorporating mindfulness into their treatment for anxiety. It requires perseverance, self-compassion, and the capacity to observe one's own feelings without evaluating or labeling them in any way. Recent research has focused on exploring both the complexities of mindfulness and the ways in which it might be useful in treating a variety of anxiety disorders. The findings of these studies shed light on the potential benefits of practicing mindfulness to reduce symptoms and improve overall wellbeing. The cultivation of a mindful attitude has emerged as a powerful ally in the battle against anxious thoughts. It is a very helpful technique for people who are looking for relief from the symptoms of anxiety because it may increase awareness, help lessen reactivity, and help cultivate emotional control. People who are looking for relief from the symptoms of anxiety will find it very helpful. The prospect that practicing mindfulness may have a beneficial effect on the management of anxiety disorders is becoming an increasingly alluring possibility as research and innovation in the field of mindfulness continue to advance.

How to get started with the practice of meditation

How to Begin Meditation: A Step in the Right Direction for Finding Peace Within Beginning a meditation practice can be a transformative event that brings about increased self-awareness, emotional fortitude, and inner calmness. Whether you are looking for relief from stress or anxiety, or simply a deeper connection with yourself, meditation provides a powerful method for cultivating mindfulness and presence in your day-to-day life. You will be guided through the fundamentals of beginning and maintaining a meditation practice with the assistance of this manual, which will also provide you with useful advice along the way.

Explanation of the Meditation Practice

Before delving into the specifics of how to meditate, a foundational understanding of the practice is essential. The contemplative practice of meditation involves training your mind to focus, becoming aware of the present moment, and developing an attitude that is nonjudgmental toward your thoughts and feelings. It is not a matter of eliminating thoughts from your head; rather, it is a matter of observing them in a dispassionate manner.

Picking Out Your Objectives

The first thing you should do when starting a meditation practice is to set your intentions. Think about why you want to meditate and write them down. Is it for the purpose of relieving stress, maintaining emotional stability, advancing spiritually, or engaging in introspection? Setting goals for yourself as you start out on your journey of meditation will help you stay motivated and focused.

Creating a Setting Appropriate for Meditation

Find a spot that is free from distractions and conducive to relaxation where you can meditate on a regular basis. It does not have to be a dedicated space; rather, it can be something as simple as a secluded nook or a section of your bedroom. Make sure there are no distractions or clutter in the area you're working in. Consider incorporating calming accessories such as candles, cushions, or artwork into your space.

Choosing a Practice for Your Meditation Routine

There is a wide variety of approaches to meditation, each of which can be customized to meet the requirements of particular goals and personal preferences. Consider some of these well-liked options that are available to you:

1. Mindfulness Meditation: This method involves paying attention to your breath, physical sensations, or a specific object while objectively observing your thoughts and emotions. This can be done by sitting in a comfortable position with your eyes closed.

2. Meditation on Loving-Kindness (Metta): The goal of Metta meditation is to cultivate feelings of self-love, compassion for others, and goodwill toward oneself and others.

3. Guided Meditation: You can find guided meditation sessions in meditation apps or have an instructor lead you through the practice. Because they provide organized guidance, they are ideal for people who are just starting out.

4. Body Scan Meditation: This type of meditation involves directing your attention to different parts of your body in order to relieve tension and promote relaxation.

5. Transcendental Meditation: Transcendental Meditation, also known as TM, is a technique that involves the use of a mantra, which can be a specific word or sound, as a point of focus in order to enter deeper states of awareness and go beyond the realm of typical thinking.

Building Mental Fortitude And Focus Will Help You Focus And Be More Resilient.

It is required to implement a mix of behavioral, physiological, and lifestyle adjustments in order to promote resilience and concentration:

1. Being in the here and now and practicing meditation

Mindfulness and meditation are two practices that can help you become more resilient, sharpen your focus, and lower your stress levels. Beginning with shorter sessions and gradually working up to longer ones is recommended.

2. Engage in Frequent Physical Activity It is recommended to engage in regular physical activity in order to boost overall brain function and concentration. Getting regular exercise not only benefits your physical and mental health but also your resilience.

3. receive Plenty of Quality Sleep: If you want to feel refreshed both physically and mentally, make sure you receive enough sleep each night. The inability to concentrate and be resilient can be caused by not getting enough sleep.

4. Eat a Variety of Foods That Are High in Fresh Produce, Whole Grains, Lean Proteins, and Other Nutrients: Consume a wide variety of foods that are high in various nutrients.

Eating healthily promotes both the resilience and health of the brain.

5. Methods for Reducing Stress In order to build resiliency, you should get familiar with methods for reducing stress, such as deep breathing, progressive muscle relaxation, or yoga.

6. Determine Precise Objectives In order to help with concentration and resiliency, as well as to provide direction and inspiration, determine specific goals for both the short term and the long term.

7. Keep Yourself Well-hydrated: If you want to be able to concentrate well and have healthy brain function, make sure you drink enough water throughout the day.

8. Minimize Distractions In order to minimize distractions, you should create a workspace that is dedicated to your job and impose limits on your usage of the phone and the internet when you are working or studying.

9. Take rests: In order to prevent burnout and maintain optimal levels of attention when working or studying, it is important to take rests at regular intervals.

10. If you are having trouble staying focused or bouncing back from setbacks, seek the

assistance of a professional in the field of mental health. They are able to offer direction and suggestions for strengthening these qualities, which is quite helpful.

Remember that cultivating resiliency and focus calls for both patience and consistent effort if you want to see results. For the greatest possible outcomes, tailor these suggestions to your individual interests and ways of living.

A Practice in Confidence in Oneself

If you have a poor self-esteem, you will have a fear of other people. You have trouble saying "no" to people when they make requests of you or expressing how you feel to other people, and you also have trouble asking for what you want. This lack of self-assurance puts one at risk, particularly when they are in a social context.

At your expense, it will be very easy for other people to get away with everything they want to do. On their way to achievement, others will use you as a stepping stone, and that success will be your reward. Training in assertiveness will equip you with new abilities that will help you to talk confidently about how you feel or what you want without worrying about the possible damage this could create to your relationships with other people.

You are concerned that being aggressive will put a strain on your relationship the majority of the time, but this will never be the case. During your sessions on assertiveness, your therapist will address the unnecessary fear that you have.

Methodology for the Resolution of Problems

If you lack confidence in yourself, you may regularly experience feelings of helplessness. Your self-confidence and capacity to overcome obstacles are constantly called into question whenever you are faced with a new obstacle. If you make an effort to resolve the issue, you worry that you won't be successful. You are anxious about the opinions of others regarding the effort that you have put forth.

Through the process of training you to effectively solve problems, your therapist will work with you to find solutions to the challenges you face. You will gain the ability to recognize optimal solutions, particularly with regard to making use of the resources that are available to you. You will learn how to muster the bravery necessary to put a solution to the problem into action and implement a strategy.

Instruction on Social Skills

Low self-esteem and a lack of social skills go hand in hand with each other. You have a hard time communicating with other people. Even with people who you ought to consider your peers, people with whom you share a lot of things in common, you have a hard time finding a place for yourself in any social circle.

Training in social skills is essential because it will teach you how to better your interactions with the people who are in your immediate environment. You will learn how to be comfortable with people, how to reward appropriate social behavior, and how to take a good attitude toward encounters.

A distorted view of one's own abilities is at the root of low self-esteem. The Cognitive Behavioral Therapy (CBT) helps you identify the underlying causes of these cognitive perceptions. It is much simpler to reframe your thought process and boost your self-esteem if you have an understanding of how you derive meaning from the circumstances in which you find yourself. Your therapist will listen to you and then assist you with refocusing many elements of your life in order to modify the patterns of behavior you exhibit.

Recognizing and Addressing Negative Self-Talk

The foundation of cognitive therapy is the idea that the way in which one thinks directly correlates to the feelings that one experiences. If you consistently dwell on unfavorable aspects of life, you will inevitably have unfavorable feelings. However, you can learn how to modify your mental process through cognitive behavioral therapy (CBT). You will be able to learn how to recognize unrealistic thought patterns and alter them into healthier ways of thinking with the assistance of your therapist. Cognitive distortions are to be found in these false patterns of cognition.

When going about their day-to-day activities, the vast majority of people deal with one or more of the following three cognitive distortions:

Syndrome of the Should

The "should syndrome" refers to the practice of establishing hard and fast guidelines for how one ought to behave when in the company of other people. It is also relevant to how you would like other people to act when they are in your presence. If you break even one of these guidelines, you will have a bad feeling about yourself. This syndrome is also accompanied by feelings of remorse. A excellent illustration of this is when something unexpected does place and you think to yourself, "I really ought to have been more prepared for this."

You need to stop wallowing in regret and start thinking about how you can adjust your expectations so that they are in line with the things you are capable of doing. It is healthy to push yourself to perform better, but you should make sure that the objectives you set for yourself are attainable at the same time. You shouldn't expect to do everything you set out to do, but you should make an effort to do so. Always make an effort to acknowledge and appreciate your own accomplishments.

The benefits of developing and maintaining effective time management skills

The effective management of one's time can result in the acquisition of a variety of benefits, some of which are listed below:

a Increased Quantity and Quality of Output

The effective management of one's time can be beneficial to the individual. When tasks are completed in a way that is more efficient, the end result is probably going to be an increase in production as well as an improvement in performance.

A Lower Overall Level of Anxiety and Stress

Efficient time management can help individuals experience less stress and worry in their day-to-day lives by providing them with a sense of control and success in the management of their time.

Balance between one's professional and personal life

Better time management can help individuals achieve a healthy balance between their personal and professional life, which can lead to increased feelings of contentment. This balance can help individuals feel more in control of their lives.

A stronger sense of having succeeded and completed the task at hand

People feel a better sense of accomplishment and satisfaction when they are able to accomplish their objectives in a manner that is more expedient thanks to excellent management of their time. This contributes to their overall sense of well-being.

The vast majority of people are aware of how important it is to improve their ability to manage their time, especially in their professional lives. The findings of a research that was conducted by Salary.com showed that 88 percent of people who were asked admitted to wasting time at their place of employment on a daily basis. The ability to effectively manage one's time is becoming increasingly difficult to achieve in today's world, what with the prevalence of things like cell phones, social media, and regular email. In spite of this, if you put these six recommendations into practice, you will be well on your way to increasing your productivity at work while simultaneously decreasing the number of interruptions you experience.

Check to see that you have prompts or reminders set up for each of your obligations.

The secret to effective time management is to make sure you are aware of all of your impending due dates and that you remind yourself of them in a timely manner. In order to ensure that there will be sufficient time for preparation and the gathering of any materials that may be required, we strongly recommend setting an alarm 15 minutes in advance of any event or meeting.

Create a plan for each day of the week.

Make a list of the things that need to get done today and make a note of any forthcoming appointments or deadlines as they come up. Create a list of the things that need to get done today. As you move through the procedure, you should be sure to check off that each step "has been accomplished" as soon as you can after completing it.

You can choose to implement any one of the following time management tactics in order to gain a better hold on how you spend your time:

Put a time restriction on each and every one of your tasks: Make a list of the tasks you have to perform each day, and give yourself a rough estimate of how much time it will take you to finish each one. If you find that you are unable to finish a task within the specified period of time, you should halt what you are doing and come back to it at a later time. The simple act of taking a break and redirecting one's attention to a different group of duties can frequently result in the development of a fresh perspective.

Turning off email notifications and setting regular periods at which you will check your inbox, such as once every two hours for a half an hour, will help you get rid of any potential sources of distraction that may be getting in the way of your work. In order to get the most work done, it is preferable to eliminate distractions that are not relevant to the task at hand. Some examples of such distractions include the use of a cell phone, participation in social media, and online shopping.

Establish a pattern of consistency: Create a schedule for yourself that is suited particularly to the requirements of the position you have. When you have a pattern that you always stick to, it is much simpler to keep things in order, figure out what your priorities are, and not put things off. In addition to this, it will reduce the amount of stress in your life and will be beneficial to your mental health.

The Role That Each Gene Plays In The Development Of The Anxiety Condition

It has been shown that some changes in a person's DNA can in fact lead to anxiety disorders in that person. However, it is vital to bear in mind that genetics are not the only factor that plays a role in deciding the outcome of an individual's mental health. Other factors that play a role in this process include environment, lifestyle, and experiences. Instead, genetic variations are deviations in a person's genetic code that can influence their susceptibility to anxiety in a number of different ways. These variances can have an effect on a person's lifetime risk of developing anxiety disorders. Due to these various factors, a person's susceptibility to anxiety might either be increased or decreased.

To begin, there is no such thing as a single "anxiety gene" that is to blame for anxiety disorders. These conditions are caused by a combination of factors. Instead, the interaction of a multitude of genes is what leads to certain disorders being present in a person. These so-called "anxiety genes" often have subtle but cumulative impacts on a person's vulnerability to anxiety, which is why they are dubbed "anxiety genes."

Second, there is evidence that the manner in which particular neurotransmitters in the brain, such as serotonin and GABA, function can be altered by variances in one's genetic makeup. These neurotransmitters are responsible for regulating not only our feelings but also our levels of anxiety as well.

Third, differences in an individual's genetic make-up can disrupt the natural equilibrium of these neurotransmitters, which can lead to an increase in anxious sensations in the individual.

The heritability of anxiety disorders has been demonstrated through studies on twins as well as families, which leads us to our fourth point, which is that genetic predispositions to anxiety disorders may be handed down through families.

People who come from families where anxiety disorders have occurred in the past have a greater risk of having a genetic predisposition that makes them more likely to develop these diseases themselves. In some people, there appears to be a genetic tendency that makes them more likely to develop anxiety problems, according to the findings of studies that involved studies of identical twins and extended families. However, it is vital to bear in mind that a person's genetics are not the only element that decides whether or not they will develop an anxiety disorder. Other factors that play a role in this process include environmental factors and social factors. Anxiety disorders can be started in people who are genetically predisposed to having the disease by environmental factors such as stress during early childhood, traumatic experiences, or chronic stress. Anxiety disorders can also be caused in people who are genetically predisposed to developing the condition.

Our comprehension of the hereditary components of anxiety disorders has been given a boost by the emerging field of epigenetics, which has added a further layer of nuance to the subject. Changes in epigenetics can influence gene expression in a way that is independent of modifications to the DNA sequence that is basic to the gene. These changes can occur in the epigenome as a result of being exposed to a stressful event or traumatic experience. These alterations have the capacity to activate or inhibit genes that are connected with anxiety, which may increase the probability of a person developing an anxiety disorder. These changes have the potential to activate or suppress genes that are associated with anxiety. Some of the medications that are used to treat anxiety, such as SSRIs, function by targeting the neurotransmitter systems that are influenced by genetic factors. This is how these medications are able to alleviate the symptoms of anxiety. These drugs work to alleviate the symptoms of anxiety in the manner described above.

Individuals who have a greater reaction to particular medications or treatments may be able to be identified through genetic testing if they are willing to undergo the process.

The fear of succeeding in what one has set out to do.

The dread of being unsuccessful has its counterpart in the opposite form, which is the fear of being successful. On the surface, the notion that someone could have fear of something going well is one that contradicts logic; yet, there is more to the concept than meets the eye. When a person is terrified of becoming successful, they are not necessarily fearful of earning a lot of money or landing the job of their dreams. Instead, they are afraid of being successful. They are more concerned about the changes that will occur in elements of themselves and their relationships as a direct result of obtaining success, such as how their personality or the dynamics of their interpersonal relationships will evolve. Additionally, they are concerned about the changes that will occur in their careers. The subconscious ideas that people have about the desirability of success are the reason why they are able to conjure up imaginary scenarios that cast success in an unflattering light. This is because of the beliefs that people have. For instance, a person might have the desire of establishing financial stability, but the possibility of raising their income might persuade them to abandon their goal and pursue the higher income instead. Why? people may have been brought up to believe that money is the root of all evil, which is a negative money view that causes them to reject down opportunities to make money. Because of this negative money belief, people may turn down opportunities to make money.

If a person is terrified of being successful in life, it is possible for them to sabotage their own efforts to achieve their goals and become successful in life. It's not that they don't believe in themselves sufficiently or that they don't have the skills or qualities that are required to be successful in their endeavors. Their major worry is that they would be put in a position where they will have to confront the challenges and hardships that come along with success. The following is a list of situations that you may probably identify with, including the following:

You want to improve your self-confidence so that you can converse with a wider range of individuals, but you're worried that other people will pay "too much" attention to you or that you'll be the focus of their attention.

You want to become an expert in your profession, but you're concerned that doing so will set you apart from those who are currently working in the same sector.

You have been wanting to own your own home for as long as you can remember, but you are concerned about the reaction of those around you to a purchase of this magnitude.

You have the desire to live an alternative lifestyle, but you are concerned that people will condemn you or look down on you for doing so. This is something that you want to do.

You have always had the objective of being a successful person, but you are worried that achieving that objective may cause an undesirable shift in your personality.

You worry that if you succeed in increasing your money, it will make you more materialistic, despite the fact that this is one of the things you want most in the world.

You have the wish to make changes to your routine or way of life, but you resist from doing so because you are afraid that doing so will cause you to become estranged from the people you care about, your friends, or your community.

It is possible to undermine your efforts to reach your objectives and live the quality of life you have always sought in your life by having what is known as the fear of success. This fear can manifest itself in the form of anxiety over either achieving or failing at something. Both of these phobias can give you the feeling that maximizing all of your potential is either risky for you or not something you should do at this time in your life.

Think about the exact things that give you anxiety in order to overcome your anxieties of achieving and failing in whatever endeavor you undertake. For instance, what is it about the possibility of being rejected or the actuality of being accepted that makes you feel anxious? Which of these two scenarios is more likely to occur? Is this the opinion that you think other people will have of you, or do you have a different perception? Or the way that success can cause your ego to get inflated and lead to negative consequences. After that, you'll be able to play some games based on the "what if" scenario. Ask yourself what steps you would take to protect yourself in the event that your worst fears came true. What would be different in this scenario? What could possibly go wrong, and more importantly, what steps could you take to improve your situation?

If you give some attention to the worst possible outcome of a situation, you will be able to better control your concerns and come up with a range of solutions to cope with stressful circumstances. In the event that you do feel an expansion of your ego, you may want to look for ways to bring yourself back down to earth, such as by engaging in the practice of gratitude or assisting others who are in need of aid. You should remind yourself that rather than focusing on the destination, you should concentrate on the route that you are taking to get there. Pay close attention to each individual phase of your comprehensive strategy, and do your best not to allow yourself to become sidetracked by the overall picture. You will find that the most substantial issues are lot easier to manage if you commit your time and effort to becoming an expert in the specifics. If you do this, you will find that this is the case.

In The Event That You Have Social Anxiety Disorder, There Are Specific Actions That You Ought To Steer Clear Of.

Recognizing that you battle with social anxiety is not something that should bring you any sense of shame. You are in no means the only person struggling with this issue; but, although there are many things that you ought to be doing, there are also some things that you have to stop doing. although there are numerous things that you ought to be doing, there are also some things that you have to stop doing.

1. Stop avoiding things and face them head-on.

There are many alternative routes one can take to avoid a certain situation. When they go to social gatherings, some people drink quite a bit only to give themselves the self-assurance they need to get through the night. Others consume alcohol just for the purpose of getting through the night. When interacting with other people, some people avoid making eye contact, while others will read out loud exactly what they've written on a piece of paper. You need to quickly put an end to the avoidance methods, regardless of what they are or how subtle they are, because in the long term, they will only make matters worse. This means that you need to put an end to them as soon as possible. This requires you to sit with a group of people rather than in a corner, accept a drink when it is offered to you by another person, and agree to go to a social event that you would never in a million years have considered going to. You have the potential to be successful in anything you put your mind to!

2. Put an end to your negative outlook on life and think more positively.

Negative thinking is a significant contributor to social anxiety disorder and is one of the primary variables that contribute to the disease. People who suffer from anxiety disorders have access to a variety of treatments, as was described previously in this paragraph. Two of these treatments, known as acceptance and commitment therapy (ACT) and cognitive-behavioral therapy (CBT), are founded on the premise of recognizing and correcting negative thought patterns. ACT is an acronym for "acceptance and commitment therapy," and CBT stands for "cognitive behavioraltherapy." If you are having problems determining how to get started, you should begin maintaining your own personal thinking diary. This will give you an indication of how much work has to be put into changing your negative thoughts because it will show you how frequently you experience negative ideas.

3. Don't Put Off Seeking Help Any Longer Than Necessary

If you suspect that you may be suffering from an anxiety condition but have not been given an exact diagnosis, it is imperative that you seek care as quickly as possible. The successful completion of this task will represent the beginning of a fresh new way of life for you, despite the fact that it is quite likely to be the most difficult step you will ever be needed to take. It is the only way to ensure that you receive the appropriate assistance, so don't put off having a conversation with your doctor about getting properly diagnosed. Doing so as soon as possible is in your best interest. If you find that your anxiety is preventing you from carrying out the necessary actions, it is a good idea to write everything down, schedule an appointment, and then give over what you have written.

4. You Must Refuse to Accept the Fallacy That There Is No Way Forward

There is always a reason to have positive expectations. It's possible that you don't think the drug will work or that you're concerned about the potential for too many adverse effects from taking it. It's likely that you believe therapy is for fragile individuals; nevertheless, when you actually stop to think about it, what do you really have to lose by giving it a shot? You owe it to yourself to get your life back on track and the best way to do so is to give the therapies for each anxiety condition that have been proven to be effective a try. This will allow you to get your life back on track. The breadth and depth of information contained in this book make it abundantly evident that there is more than one approach to therapy that can be utilized in the treatment of seasonal affective disorder (SAD). Do not give up simply because the first option you attempted did not work. There is probably more than one answer to this problem. You shouldn't allow a negative experience in the past keep you from exploring other possibilities because it's possible that the next one you try will turn out to be the greatest option for you. Because of this possibility, you shouldn't let a bad experience in the past prohibit you from exploring other options.

5. Put an end to drawing unhelpful comparisons between yourself and other people.

You are the only one who can be you. You should never feel good about comparing yourself to other people because you are not that other person, and the only time you will ever feel good about doing so is when you are doing better than they are. This is the one time in your life when you will feel good about acting in this manner. Get used to the thought that there will always be someone who is more socially competent than you are, who has more friends than you do, or who has more confidence than you do. Acclimate yourself to this idea. Learn to accept the fact that there will always be someone else who is more self-assured than you are and make it a part of your mindset. Instead of wasting time and effort comparing your performance to that of others, focus on ways in which you may improve yourself. The most accurate measure of how well you are doing is how well you are doing in contrast to where you were one month, six months, or a year ago. This can be done monthly, quarterly, or annually. Not in the context of how you judge yourself in comparison to everyone else in your surroundings.

6. You need to quit trying to persuade yourself that you are unable to make any changes.

It is possible that you feel as though you were dealt a lousy hand, or that you may assume that you are simply too old to want assistance at this point in your life. Both of these thoughts are common. You have to immediately stop whatever it is that you're doing, and it doesn't matter what reasons you have to justify it. There is always room for change, and everyone is capable of making it; all you need to do is recognize the things that you can alter and then make those changes, while accepting the things that you can't change at the same time. The greatest method to improve social skills is to put them into practice, and gaining the appropriate kind of experience will help you feel more at ease when you have to perform in front of others or in other social contexts.

There are some people in this world who are open to new experiences and points of view, but the vast majority of people who suffer from seasonal affective disorder

(SAD) have problems adapting to new situations because of the numerous unknowns that come along with them. Some people in this world are open to new experiences and points of view. If you don't think you have the ability to make changes in your life, reading through your notebook should be enough to convince you otherwise. If you have been keeping your journal with the utmost attention to detail, there is little question that its pages will contain evidence of the progress you have made.

7. Put an end to people assuming you won't be successful and forecasting it.

Simply due to the fact that the larger your involvement in something, the higher the risk that you would eventually fail at it. Instead of brooding on the conditions under which you would rather certain events not take place, direct your focus to the occurrence of the things that you would like to see happen. If you are going to be giving a speech, you should try to see yourself as confident and outgoing. This will help you deliver a better performance. If you are compelled to attend a social function, try to imagine yourself as a person who is outgoing and sociable by nature. This will help you feel more comfortable in social situations. Even if these things do not materialize, at the very least you will be able to say that you attempted them and that you gave yourself every opportunity, even if the attempt was unsuccessful.

8. You have to stop squandering opportunities by not taking advantage of them.

Have you ever been offered a promotion at your place of employment and decided against accepting it? You haven't left the house in a very long time despite having lots of possibilities to do so, so did you drop a class at the university, or is it just that you haven't left the house in a very long time? If this describes you, then you are allowing your social anxiety disorder to take control of your life, and as a result, you are missing out on opportunities that could have been beneficial to you. When you look back on your life, you are going to have a lot of regrets about the things you didn't try or the things you didn't do that you wish you had done. You will at least have the satisfaction of knowing that you tried your best and gave it your all, and this will be true even if you are unsuccessful. Do not give in to the temptation of letting your anxiety illness run your life and stop you from doing the things that you have set out to do because of it.

9. Stop Making an Attempt to Cover Up Your Mental Illness. People who suffer from social anxiety disorders often give off the impression that they are ashamed of themselves. You are petrified that other people will suddenly learn that you suffer from anxiety and that it inhibits your ability to perform regularly in social circumstances. Furthermore, you are scared that they will find out that it prevents you from being able to function normally. Why is it necessary to keep it a secret? To get started, you should start by being honest with yourself and with other people. It is not required to approach a stranger and reveal that you have social anxiety disorder; however, if you are able to do so, you should pat yourself on the back because it reveals that you have triumphed over a large obstacle. If you are able to do so, you should pat yourself on the back because it demonstrates that you have overcome a significant obstacle. You can, however, talk about your worries with the people who are closest to you; simply explain to them what stresses you out the most. They won't make fun of you or point the finger at you; instead, they will go out

of their way to help you, and one day you might even feel comfortable enough with them to tell them all of your secrets. They won't make fun of you or point the finger at you.

Put An End To The Delusion That You Are The Only One Who Is Going Through This.

Because sufferers of anxiety disorders spend so little time engaging with other people, it is possible for them to be oblivious that those around them also struggle with challenges. This is one of the most major problems linked with anxiety disorders. You could be under the impression that everyone in your immediate environment emanates self-assurance whenever they are in a social atmosphere; however, a substantial portion of them do not. You are not the only person going through this struggle; there are many people who go through what you are going through. Talk to those individuals who go through what you are going through or read the tales of other people so that you can realize that you are not the only one going through this struggle. All that is asked of you is to look about at your surroundings. People who suffer from anxiety disorders have access to a wide variety of support groups, and signing up for one of these organizations could turn out to be one of the wisest decisions you've ever made in your life.

How to Regain Command of Your Mind and Stop Dwelling on the Negative

When you allow yourself to think negatively, your mind will be stimulated in the same way that the monkey in my circumstance was. When a person concentrates their attention on how overweight they appear in the mirror, neural connections in the brain are developed that lend credence to the notion that the person is overweight.

Continued development of a network of ideas that can communicate with one another is being carried out by the branches and networks of your nerves. This is done with the hopes that, at some point in the future, your mind will once again consider these concepts to be true. This concept is reflected in a proverb that is commonly used in the field of neurology and which reads as follows: "the nerves that fire together, wire together."

Every one of your concepts, which can be compared to a movie in some ways, has a subject. Which one of these do you believe is most in line with the most important aspect of the realization of your dreams? Which is more important: looking back at the past, living in the present, or looking forward to the future? Is it your sexual life, your personal connections, your career, your financial status, or your overall health, or is it something else different? How much of one's time does one waste by worrying about unimportant things to the point where they feel worn out? It may feel as though you are suffocating in a pit from which there is no escape; instead, it may feel as though you are sinking deeper and deeper into the pit. As was discussed before, if you don't allow the thoughts any area to stand, you can have a jump start on breaking the cycle. This was discussed farther up in the article. Try not to give your thoughts any more fuel in the shape of a feeling that is comparable to what they are experiencing.

There is a rationale behind the dismal feelings that you have been having recently. What are some of the reasons that this could be happening? What exactly is it that they want you to take away from their negative thoughts and how can you make use of this information? One of the disquieting concepts that gives me reason to be concerned is the question "what if you fail and are never able to fulfill your mission and dream?" This is one of the ideas that gives me reason to feel afraid. The mere consideration of these ideas is enough to get my heart racing since they imply that a significant amount of responsibility for determining the course of my life rests on my shoulders. The dismal scenery serves as a constant reminder to me that in order to exist in the here and now, rather than in the future, I need to be able to adjust my behavior on a daily basis. In the premise, a call to action is made to change the habit of negative thinking that you have been engaging in and to never give up. You are going to be responsible for or required to carry out this activity.

The waves of negative ideas that are washing over your head are similar to the way an infection would spread across a community. You have a strategy to "whatever," as well as a method to look for something that will enter your soul, and both of these things are in your possession. When a force is already traveling in the direction that you want it to move, what action is going to be the least difficult to take? Energy is being put to good use, which goes hand in hand with flow. In order to become a thinker, the first step is to develop some degree of intellectual discipline and stick to it. In my opinion, the simplest action you can take at this stage is to just become aware of the feelings that are currently occupying your mind. Take careful note of the amount of time (you might find that maintaining a diary is beneficial in this regard). The issue with one's thoughts, to be specific, and the question of whether or not they contain any truth. Which idea stands in such stark contrast to that one, and what is it?

If the thief demanded money from the person working behind the counter, would the person working behind the counter take the weapon away from the robber? It is possible that it is not. It would be easier for the dealer to give in to his demand and hand over the money, which would also satisfy his immediate need. You will be requested to study and evaluate your feelings by having them brought to the forefront of your mind when the criteria for a thief have been met, which means that action will be taken, which means that the police will be called.

This is a visually beautiful piece that draws inspiration from various schools of Buddhist thought. What kind of things are you thinking about? Who exactly is thinking about this? You even use the first person, saying "I" think, which is somewhat unusual. What is it that you are aware of, independent of what you believe? Show that you can do it! Show that you can do it! When I last saw you, I strongly suggested that you give some thought to the question of who is watching who. Who is the observer being watched by? You question the ideas without becoming overly worked up over the puzzles, and as a consequence, you shorten the cycle.

There is a possibility that the brain is a very intricate organ. It has a soft spot in its heart for models. It is interested in learning new things, such as where they are located and why and how they function. Make fun of it like a child might by playing a prank on it. I was able to con it. It will eventually give up and leave as a result of this because you did not stoke the flame by adopting its mind process in sufficient amounts of effort and patience. Even after you have given up on it, your mind will continue to torment you with negative thoughts, but they won't have as much of an impact on you emotionally.

www.ingramcontent.com/pod-product-compliance
Lightning Source LLC
Chambersburg PA
CBHW052143110526
44591CB00012B/1841